A Lifetime of Experience

I am pleased to recommend Mark Cole a a proven leader in the Body of Christ. You will find his unique insights on life and ministry very helpful as he shares – not just from theory, but from a lifetime of experience.

~ **Dick Iverson;** four  *ters*
Fellc ·on
An Inv

Mark has managed to t _____ with a huge amount of practical, spiritua. ...ıd very necessary insights into Worship ministry. Each point is illustrated with valuable wisdom and personal examples from his years of experience. Mark has proven to be one of the "fathers" of Worship ministry, and yet his writing is fresh and current.

I am honored to recommend this book to Worship ministers, pastors and worshippers of all denominations and generations. It is one of those "must-read" titles that will prove to be an invaluable resource for your Worship personnel, time and time again. Good for you, Mark ... this is an excellent read!

~ **Vivien Hibbert;** co-founder of *The Worship Arts Conservatory,* author, musician, speaker, Worship minister; Texarkana, Arkansas

Rediscover the Beauty of Worship

The subjects of Worship and Music in the church has been such a point of discussion and even contention in the contemporary church. Mark's heart, experience and knowledge as a worshipper and as a Worship Pastor makes this book an informative, yet exciting adventure that helps enhance and rediscover the beauty of the corporate and personal worship experience with God.

~ **Alvin Slaughter;** award-winning Worship leader, songwriter, speaker, author; Orchard Park, New York

Live a Life of Worship

There is nothing like a great story fused with the spirit of adventure! I remember hanging around Mark at his home in the early days of *PraiseCharts,* often mesmerized by his unique grasp on life, ministry, Music, Worship, marriage, and family. It seemed like every detail was intentional. Those were the days when I started to think about what I could do with my life. Maybe I could break out of my own box ... maybe, just maybe, I could do anything! The heart and life of Worship was percolating inside of me.

God has given Mark amazing experiences to share, from the mountain tops to the valleys – literally and figuratively. When you read these stories and sense his heart, you'll be inspired to dream again. Breathe in the fresh air of your own adventure, and live out a life of Worship in spirit and truth.

~ **Ryan Dahl;** CEO of *PraiseCharts;* Langley, British Columbia, Canada

Multi-Faceted Yet Single-Minded

Mark and I go back over 40 years. We first met in Japan, at the start of a 5-month missions trip with *Living Sound.* Mark was already displaying his versatility – or what I call multi-faceted-ness. On that musical tour, Mark played saxophone, flute, clarinet, keyboards, sang vocals, and gave his testimony. Not only does Mark play several instruments well (he's added guitar, harmonica and other instruments to his musical arsenal), he enjoys a wide variety of musical styles: classical, black Gospel, jazz, and much more.

Mark is both an excellent leader and an enthusiastic team player, switching from one role to another almost effortlessly. When Mark is part of the band, he is always encouraging others; when he is leading Worship, he sets the pace with his infectious combination of heart, precision and enthusiasm. His curiosity and love for life continues to open new doors and provides interesting experiences all the time.

Mark Cole has something to say. It's about time he writes a book! As I fully expected – although he is generous in sharing – Mark is quite modest and not egotistical about his impressive list of achievements. All of us can learn from a successful life like Mark's.

~ **Michael Leon Gossett;** musician, songwriter, author; Abbotsford, British Columbia

Glean From a Devoted Servant

Mark has served the Lord for many years in leading Worship, leading people, and loving Jesus. Glean from a life devoted to loving Jesus and obeying His Word.

~ **Bob Sorge;** author, *bobsorge.com*; Kansas City, Missouri

Enabling Better-Equipped Leaders

I have known Mark for 30 years, and have admired his talent, his passion, his heart for the things of God, and his longing to see people saved. I have called on Mark's arranging abilities many times over the years and have always received a professional product, on time. He is a respected Worship Leader, leading services in several countries around the world, as well as serving in Canadian churches, with a reputation for excellence. He is a family man, an adventurist, and has created a Bucket List that contains an unforgettable point: a personal desire to see one-million people accept Christ.

His writings reflect on these various life experiences in a way that all of us can relate. In his book, Mark inspires us to create, to grow, to dream, to teach, to experience, to love, and to pray. This material will be a go-to for many of us, and we look for quick, practical and time-tested solutions to common issues which we, as Worship Leaders, face. Every topic causes us to consider the application in a personal way. Mark's well-balanced approach allows for us to be inspired physically, mentally, emotionally, and spiritually as individuals, enabling us to be better-equipped leaders.

~ **Blaine Eagle;** Senior Associate Pastor and Music Pastor, *Elim Church*; Saskatoon, Saskatchewan, Canada

An Invaluable Tool for Any Worshipper

For over 40 years, I have had the privilege of watching Mark Cole exemplify the life of Worship. From his overseas' missions trips, to traveling in bands, to playing multiple instruments with concert-level skill, to leading my high school choir in competitions, and, of course, leading Worship in church – it has been a personal privilege to see what the heart of God looks like in the flesh.

The wisdom of a lifetime of experience in service to the King has been recorded now as a legacy to every man and woman who finds his or her heart yearning to be a true worshipper. Mark's expertise in song writing, musical proficiency, team support, and leadership will elevate and advance your aptitude immediately.

What you will learn about a true heart of Worship through Mark's quest for excellence in purity of heart, and his exceptional transparency as a man in search of the very presence of God – will teach your soul intimacy with Jesus. This book is an invaluable tool for any budding or experienced Worship leader. The hidden secrets and lessons learned through thousands of hours of honing his craft are now handed to you as an added instrument in your armory to bring glory to God. For some who desire to find a deeper walk, the stories and intricate weaving of God's destiny through Mark's life will bless you. This book is a must-have for those who are called to the awesome responsibility of leading humanity into the manifest inner court of the place God inhabits: our Praise and Worship.

~ **Laura-Lynn Tyler Thompson;** co-host for *The 700 Club Canada;* Vancouver, British Columbia

An Uncommon Passion for Worship

What an honor it is for us to write a recommendation for this book. Mark Cole is one of the most gifted Worship leaders in the world today. He has made a tremendous impact around the world with his uncommon passion for Worship and his great leadership which has been an inspiration to us and the team over the many years he have known him.

The humor in his stories will make you remember the lessons, and the lessons will greatly improve your effectiveness in ministry and in life. Overall, this book is an enjoyable and informative read, and will definitely bless you. We highly recommend this book for those who are ready to move on to a new dimension in life and ministry.

~ **Apostle Charles** and **Pastor Donna Ndifon;** co-founders of *Christ Love Ministries International;* Johnston, Rhode Island

This Is a Must-Read

I have lived with Mark through many of these wonderful stories. I am excited to see him share what he has learned with worshippers and leaders around the world. I believe these stories will be your go-to guide for years to come. This is a must-read for Worship leaders and worshippers alike.

~ **Anna Cole,** wife of Mark Cole; fund-developer; Calgary, Alberta

LEADING WORSHIP

Notes From A Grand Adventure

Mark Cole

LEADING WORSHIP
Notes From a Grand Adventure

By **Mark Cole,** B.Music

Edited by **Jeanne Halsey**

ISBN 978-1-312-44812-4

LEADING WORSHIP: Notes From a Grand Adventure by **Mark M. Cole** (1954 –); edited by Jeanne M. Halsey; copyright © 2014; published by **New Dream Press,** a division of *GT Music Publishing House;* ISBN 978-1-312-44812-4.

Unless otherwise stated, all Scripture quotations are taken from the *Holy Bible, New Living Translation* ® (NLT); copyright © 1996, 2004,

For more information, contact:

Mark Cole
mark.cole@mac.com
www.markcole.ca

TABLE OF CONTENTS

Part One: NOTES FROM A GRAND ADVENTURE

Part Two: LEADING WORSHIP and GROWING TEAMS

DEDICATION

I dedicate this book to my beautiful Italian bride, **Anna** (*née* Foti) **Cole.** We recently celebrated 31 awesome years of marriage. She has been such a huge support through all the ups and downs of ministry and travel. She epitomizes the servant's heart; I couldn't have asked for a better life-partner. She has given me two great children, who in turn have married wonderful partners, and have since given us two amazing grandchildren (so far). I am blessed. *"I love you, Amore!"*

FOREWORD
By **Howard Rachinski**

"To know wisdom and instruction, to perceive the words of understanding ..."

How fitting are these words uttered from the son of the Psalmist in Proverbs 1:2. Solomon's father, King David, is considered to be the "flagship" and the "fixed point" of all we strive for in the wonderful realm of Worship. As founder of *Christian Copyright Licensing International* (CCLI), as well as being actively involved in church and Worship leadership for over four decades, it has been my privilege to participate and interact with many thousands of churches, pastors and Worship leaders around the world. I have been blessed (I think) to have observed styles, trends and influences of music and Christian movements that have – like wave after wave – filled, flooded and overwhelmed church Worship.

"Worship wars," generational preferences, technology, staging, and musical complexities seem to sometimes override the simple essence of our spiritual journey: *"O come, let us worship and bow down, let us kneel before the LORD our Maker"* (Psalm 95:6). Although our opinions may convince us that these aspects have only arisen over the past few decades – they haven't. In the midst of King David's delightful expressions of Worship, creation of instruments and establishing an "order" of presentation, he also had to wade through the clutter of Worship digressions (remember the cart?), character issues and a plethora of questions – *who? how? where? when? what?* – regarding entering the LORD's presence. The subject of Worship is a volatile within this church today. Many leaders have questions and concerns, many leaders have frustrations and anxieties, many leaders feel helpless and are desperate ... and it's all about Worship.

In the midst of the questions, concerns, frustrations, anxieties, helplessness, and desperation, the words from the Prophet Amos seem to be very timely:

> *"I've had all I can take of your noisy ego-music. When was the last time you sang to Me?"*
> **Amos 5:23;** the Message

This is why I like what Mark has captured in this book. I have known Mark all my life – well, I should, because he's my cousin. We grew up in the same church, participated in a great music ministry together, and together experienced the incredible blessing of worshipping the Lord in a Presence-filled congregation.

I had the joy of "baptizing" my cousin into some fun-filled antics. Like putting him in his mother's clothes dryer along with some pillows, tumble-drying him ... and telling him it was an amusement park ride. And having Mark as my "brakeman" on a very unsafe, home-made go-kart, speeding out of control down our backyard lane. Yes, the brakes didn't work; yes, the crash was brutal; and yes, we experienced severe cases of road rash!

I have also had the joy of ministering side-by-side with my cousin. Through his 40-plus years of Music and Worship ministry, I have seen Mark become a statesman, an ambassador and a mentor in this precious calling.

When a person first begins their journey in Worship ministry, you tend to think it is a 100-yard dash: you enthusiastically exude creativity and unabated energy. After awhile, you begin to think it is really a one-mile race: you try to pace your inspiration and energy lap-by-lap. After a few more years, you become convinced it's really a marathon: your initial surge of exhilaration has long ago dissipated, pangs of numbness and exhaustion belabor you, but you steadfastly plod through. But after wisdom has finally embraced you, you realize it was never a 100-yard dash, nor a one-mile race, nor a marathon – your Worship ministry has always been a **relay!** For you received the "baton" of your calling from the generation before you, you run with it during your season, and you are to pass the baton of your calling to the generation that follows you. That's what King David also discovered when he sang: *"One generation shall praise Your works to another"* (Psalm 145:4).

Oliver Wendell Holmes, Sr., said: *"For the simplicity on this side of complexity, I wouldn't give you a fig. But for the simplicity on the other side of complexity, for that I would give you anything I have."* Mark Cole's book, *"Leading Worship: Notes From a Grand Adventure,"* graciously ushers us past the complexity and into the simplicity of worshipping the Lord. Mark's 40-plus years of experience has enabled him to provide us with wisdom and understanding regarding Worship. It is practical, it is clear, it is real. His book will help you stay in the "lanes" of the relay and run with the calibration of truth so that you too may achieve the prize of the high calling:

I press on to reach the end of the race, and receive the heavenly prize for which God, through Christ Jesus, is calling us.

Philippians 3:14

Mark Cole is passing the baton of his calling to you. Like Mark, may this book help you to run with the baton of your calling to your generation, so you may pass it on to the generations who follow.

Mark originally wrote this book as blogs posted on his website and FaceBook; that's why it's mostly quick and easy to read. But never doubt that there's serious meat in them — so after you eat and begin to digest them, allow God to speak to you through Mark's heart for Worship.

* * *

Howard Rachinski is Founder and Chairman/CEO of Christian Copyright Licensing International, Inc. *(CCLI), who provide the Church Copyright License and other resources that help churches comply with the Copyright Law. Howard has experience as a songwriter, arranger, record producer, and music sales manager. He is an experienced seminar leader, and serves on the Executive Leadership Team of* City Bible Church *in Portland, Oregon. Howard has been married to his wife Donna for over 41 years. They have three children and five grandchildren (with more to come!). The Rachinskis reside in the Portland, Oregon, area.*

INTRODUCTION

Recently I had one of those "*Ah-ha*" moments: I suddenly realized I had been doing Music and Worship full-time for forty years. Forty years ... unbelievable!

I admire people who are passionate about what they do. Whether your passion is business, sports, counseling, speaking, cooking — whatever it is, I love people who are passionate! People who live life to the fullest.

I have been passionate about Music and Worship since I was a kid. I was one of those kids who loved taking Music lessons. I was one of those kids who loved singing, worshipping and playing music in church. I have never lost that passion.

That passion has taken me to over 60 countries: leading, playing, singing, and speaking in front of millions of people. That passion has led me to produce 20 recording projects, 25 musicals, and write over 1,000 music arrangements and orchestrations. That passion has led me to selling over a million dollars worth of Praise and Worship charts on *PraiseCharts.com*. That passion has allowed me to see hundreds of thousands of people from all over the world come to know Jesus as their Savior. That passion has led me to 30 years of leading Worship and pastoring in local churches.

I love the local church. I love working in the local church. I have worked in small churches, medium churches, and large churches. I have a great fondness and respect for the local church musicians. It is fun and exciting to travel around the world, but the local church is where the main ministry of Music and Worship is done. The local church is where we train up the next generation of musicians. The local church is where the job of discipleship really happens.

This book is mainly about Music and Worship in the local church. I have included stories from my travels because fun and crazy things happen on the road. But my main goal is to impart a little wisdom to the next generation coming up. To share a little wisdom with the volunteer, part-time and full-time Worship Pastor who has been at it for a few years and is still trying to figure out church ministry.

This book — which is not written chronologically — is about my desire to love the Lord with all my heart. It is about seeing the faithfulness and goodness of God over a lifetime. It is about trying to live out the great advice:

Trust in the LORD *with all your heart, and do not lean on your own understanding.   In all your ways, acknowledge Him, and He will direct your paths.*

Proverbs 3:5-6

Mark Cole
Calgary, Alberta, Canada
September 2014

Part One: NOTES FROM A GRAND ADVENTURE

I have seen God work in amazing ways my whole life. He has opened incredible doors that I could never have opened. He has allowed me to experience miracles and supply that were beyond my abilities. Before I get into what I have learned about Worship ministry, let me tell you a few stories about God's goodness and faithfulness in my life.

1: GOD ANSWERED MY PRAYER FOR A WIFE, AND MORE

In the autumn of 1981, I was traveling in Europe as the Music Director for *Living Sound III*. I was 27 years old, had completed my Bachelor of Music Degree, and had traveled in over 30 countries telling the message, through Music, of Jesus' love and forgiveness. That season, our team was supposed to go back behind the Iron Curtain for three weeks of concerts in Portland, but because of "Solidarity strikes" in Poland, all our concerts were canceled. We ended up staying the month of October at a *Youth With A Mission* hostel not too far from Vienna, Austria.

At that time, God was working in my life to clean up some of the inconsistencies in my Christian walk (read: "sin"). I have found that whenever God wants to go to the next level in my walk with Him, He will challenge inconsistencies in my life. I was challenged by a friend to read through my Bible ... and once I started reading the Bible, it seemed like I couldn't put it down. God used those weeks in Austria to soften and change my heart and make His Word so real to me! I remember sensing His love and power as I spent many hours each day reading the Bible. I ended up reading the whole Bible in three and a half months. It was then that I made a commitment to the Lord to read the Bible every single day – that was over 30 years ago, and it still is my habit to this day.

But I digress. Another thing I did in Austria was to watch a video by a New Zealand teacher, Winkie Pratney, on *"How to Find a Wife."* His teaching was based on the story of Abraham sending his servant to find a wife for Isaac, Abraham's son (see Genesis 24). The servant prayed that he would find *"a woman who would water camels."* The core of Winkie's teaching is that the servant prayed specifically and asked for *"a woman with a servant's heart."* Drawing water from a well for many camels to drink was a lot of work!

That sounded good to me, so I drew up a list of 19 things that I was looking for in a wife. I was very specific. I prayed for my future wife's exact age, hair color, relationship with her father, relationship with God, and a host of other details – including that she would be a *"a woman who waters camels"* or *"a woman with a servant's heart."* I still have that list in one of my old Bibles.

Over the next few months, God continued to work on my heart and transform me. I don't know how much other people noticed, but I felt like a totally new person – and I great passionate about reading and memorizing God's Word.

When that *Living Sound* tour was finishing in early 1982, I got a surprise phone call from my home church in Vancouver, British Columbia. They wanted me to come home to write and conduct music for their 120-voice choir and orchestra. I really had doubts about whether I could do it, but I felt like God was calling me back home.

When I was home and learning how to conduct the choir and lead people (many whom were twice my age), I noticed this cute Italian girl, **Anna Foti**, singing in the choir. I wasn't in a big hurry to start a relationship, but I did slowly get to know her through some double-dates. As I became better acquainted with Anna, I realized that she was meeting **all** of my 19 prayer requests – it was time to get married! God was answering my prayer! I had been scared of marriage my whole life (it is a huge commitment), but now it was time.

We were married the next year, in February 1983 ... and this last February, we celebrated our 31st wedding anniversary on a cruise in the Caribbean. We now have two great children, who married wonderful Christians ... and we now have two awesome grandchildren. Anna Foti Cole has been God's answer for me. I am truly blessed!

2: THE EYES OF THE LORD

Sitting in a Conference many years ago, I remember hearing a preacher talk about a verse from 2 Chronicles 16:9 –

The eyes of the LORD search the whole Earth in order to strengthen those whose hearts are fully committed to Him.

It was a fascinating sermon. It is so cool that God is looking for men and women who are totally committed to Him. God is looking for people whom He can support and strengthen.

I have always been aware that God watches over me, have always had a sense of God-awareness. When I was a young boy helping my father build church pews for our new church building, I accidentally put my right arm down on a running wood-planer. It could easily have severed my tendons, but the sweater I was wearing jammed the machine – and I didn't get a scratch because God's angels were watching over me.

A few years later, when I was 12, my father was killed in an industrial accident. I remember the utter shock when Grandma Cole came to the house and told us he was gone. I recall the days of tears and bewilderment, yet I always knew God was watching over me.

This did not mean I was always perfect. When I did stupid things, God would find a way to bring me back into line. When I was going through hard times, the piano was my place to spend time with God. I would sit in the basement of my parents' home late into the evening, playing for hours. I guess in some ways, it was like David playing his harp to the LORD: I have noticed lately that many of David's best psalms were written when he was going through terrible times. I have also found that some of my best songs have come when I am going through a rough patch.

It is not only God Who watches us, but other people watch us also. After one very busy Easter season, when I had put in long hours producing an Easter musical, I was sitting on an airplane going to a conference and just catching up on my Bible reading. I was trying to get back on track with my *"read through the Bible in a year"* plan. Little did I know there was a pastor sitting a few rows behind me on the airplane. He had recognized me but **Pastor Johnson** decided not to let me know he and his wife were there; he decided to just watch what I was doing. Fortunately, all I did was read my Bible. He later told my pastor, **Don**

Cantelon, what he had observed. I got some undeserved "brownie points" that day!

During all my travels (over 65 countries, at this point), I've always been aware God has been watching over me, He was there to strengthen me. Through all the weird twists and turns of my life, there's always been this abiding sense that God was there ... that I should not worry ... that God **is** with me.

3: IN PRAISE OF THE LEADERS OF MY YOUTH

Previously I mentioned all the musical mentors from my journey. This week, as I was sitting in church, I was reminded of my first pastor. That pastor has influenced my life more than any other.

When I was born in Vancouver, **Reg Layzell** was pastor of our church, *Glad Tidings*. Pastor Layzell was my pastor through the first 16 or 17 years of my life. One of my fondest memories of Pastor Layzell was when – after my Dad passed away – he took me to his vacation home on Keat's Island for a week. Spending time fishing and boating with him and another friend, **Grant Livingstone,** was great.

Pastor Layzell was very big on prayer, giving, missions, and Worship. If you were in the *Glad Tidings* choir or orchestra, it was mandatory to be in the Prayer Room a half-hour before the Sunday night service. He also taught the importance of tithing, and of supporting missions work. *Glad Tidings* was also a great church to learn about worshipping God. Some very strong Worship leaders came out of that church.

Pastor Layzell was also a strong supporter and promoter of **Kids' Camp.** As a kid, I had many great summers camping, boating, canoeing, playing baseball, going to Chapel, playing in the worship band, hiking, singing around campfires. They were such influential days.

I first learned I was a leader at Kids' Camp. One summer, I was put in charge of one of the four camp sports teams; our team came in first place. The next year, I was put in charge again, and our team won again. I had never considered myself a leader before that.

Kids' Camp was also the place where I developed a closer relationship with God: memorizing Scripture, praying at the altar, writing notes from our daily classes, and worshipping God with all my heart during our Chapel sessions. They were special times in a young man's life!

Many thanks to Pastor Layzell, and all the pastors and camp leaders in my life and the lives of other campers. Thanks to **Lou and Marion Peterson, Wayne Stilling, Bob Hoggard, Dan Burr, Kevin Preston,** and so many others.

4: MY CHRISTIAN HERITAGE

I am so blessed: I have Christian grandfathers
and grandmothers on both sides of my family.
It was great to have been brought up by parents
and grandparents who had Christian principles
and morals. Parents and grandparents who knew
the importance of regular church attendance and
prayer. Christians are not always perfect, but they
do understand God's love and grace.

My maternal-grandfather **Julius Rachinski**
was a German pastor who pioneered a number of
churches across Canada. He was a carpenter by
trade, who loved to teach people about Jesus. As
a result – on the Rachinski side of the family –
there are quite a number of pastors and music
pastors. It is so good to have a Christian heritage.

Grampa Rachinski was also a builder,
constructing many churches and houses. When
he was 90, he built the house in which his wife
still lives. When he was in his 80s, he was still
teaching Bible classes at the church he pioneered
in East Vancouver. My only regret about Grampa
Rachinski is that I never heard him preach – he
only preached in German, and I only understand
English.

I also have many fond memories of my paternal grandfather **David Levi Cole.** Grampa Cole was the head butcher at *Woodwards* (a former Canadian department store). I remember many great Sunday lunches after church – Grampa Cole knew how to do a roast dinner! He had been a cook in the *Canadian Army,* and we were blessed to have great meals whenever we visited his house. He also had a great garden at the back of his Richmond house. I can still remember the fresh peas, carrots and corn on the cob. So good, so good!

All my grandparents were good people, but I was closest to my **Grandma Velma Cole.** I love what my cousin **Velma Taylor** said about her: *"We had the best grandma in the world. Some people ask, 'What would Jesus do?' but I find myself asking, 'What would Grandma Cole do?' because she loved Jesus."*

Another cousin, **David Ferencz,** has an awesome story about Grandma Cole's last day on Earth: *"A few hours before Grandma passed away, she phoned me. She said she was feeling a little more tired lately. I said I would probably be out to see her Sunday afternoon, and added something to the effect of 'Don't be sad or lonely.' But Grandma replied, 'Oh, I am so happy and blessed! I can hear the angels singing right now!' As we hung up, I told her I loved her one last time. I wouldn't have made it this far without her."*

There are now five living generations on both sides of my family. It's great to see pastors, musicians, missionaries, TV hosts, successful Christian business men, and other Godly men and women on both sides. We are not a perfect family, but we are a family who loves God, and His love for us always seems to bring us back to the center.

> *Blessed are those who fear the LORD, who find great delight in His commands. Their children will be mighty in the land; the generation of the upright will be blessed. Wealth and riches are in their houses, and their righteousness endures forever.*
>
> **Psalm 112:1-3**

I thank the Lord for my Christian heritage!

5: CAN YOU REALLY TRUST GOD?

Have you ever come to a crossroads in your life and wondered if you can really trust God to show you the right way? Will God deliver on His promise to direct your path?

God always has better plans for me than I have had for myself. When I was 18 and wondering about what my life's occupation would be, I was sure I would be a school Music teacher. God, however, had other plans: He wanted me to travel and use my musical abilities in evangelism. Later, when I turned 30, God directed my path to lead Worship in a church. I had never considered leading Worship, but again, God knew me better than I know myself.

Later, in my 40s, I thought I would write Music full-time for a living, and stop leading Worship. God had other plans: He wanted me to travel again and lead Worship all over the world. He wanted me to be involved with seeing thousands of people accept Jesus, and to see some amazing miracles and healings. God has always had a better plan for my life than I have!

My life's verse – that Bible passage which God brings to my memory again and again – is Proverbs 3:5-6 –

Trust in the LORD with all your heart, and don't lean on your own understanding. In all your ways, acknowledge Him, and He will direct your paths.

God has shown me, time after time, that He will direct my paths. If I try to figure things out using my own wisdom, I am invariably wrong. I have learned that God wants me to trust Him and acknowledge Him in everything I do (to put Him in first place in all my activities). He has promised to show me the right path from there.

I love the part of the verse that says, *"Don't lean on your own understanding."* That is often very hard for me to do! My human mind wants to figure out things for myself, to make my own goals and plans. But I've learned that God's goals and plans are so much better than mine.

So take my advice: trust God. When you get to a crossroad in your life, learn to trust what God is saying to you. Seek Him, spend time reading His Word, pray, maybe even fast. God really does have a better plan for your life than you can imagine!

6: SECRETS TO GETTING TO THE TOP

A few years ago, I climbed the largest mountain in our area. *Mount Temple* is the highest peak (3,543 meters or 11,624 feet) in the Canadian Rockies, that you can scramble (you don't have to use ropes). I had never climbed that high before, so I was looking forward to the challenge.

The small team I hiked with wanted to be successful, so most of us did all the necessary training and preparation we could. We spent the summer hiking small mountains, and got in reasonably good shape. We read all we could about the best time of year to hike, and the best route to get to the top of Mount Temple.

We got to the Mount Temple area the evening before, and stayed overnight in a hostel so we could get an early start. By this time, those who had trained properly were experienced hikers who knew what was needed to be successful: we had helmets to protect us from falling rock ... we had great hiking boots ... we had proven climbing clothes with multiple layers to prepare us for the change in temperatures we would experience going to the top ... we packed enough water, food and rations to look after us for the day, but not too much to weigh us down. Most of us were prepared!

Most of us had a great day due to our training, experience and preparation. The weather was phenomenal. All our equipment and supplies were perfect for the day, and our core team made it up and down in record time. What a great (but tiring) day! Although, for the record, only three of our six climbers made it to the top – between the daunting short rock climbs and the tough cardio – it was too tough for the ones who had not trained properly.

In life, we will often encounter mountains. How prepared are you? What are you doing to keep yourself in spiritual, mental and physical shape? Life is a bit different for everyone, but I will tell you what works for me.

Spiritually

I **spend time with God every day.** I read the Bible and other great inspirational books and blogs. I love to spend time with my wife and family. I go to church on a weekly basis to honor God and become inspired by fellow Christians. I also hang out with good friends and athletes who inspire and challenge me.

Mentally

I work at what I am passionate about! I am a musician, so I practice and write music on a daily basis. Did you know that Music is one of the few brain activities that uses all parts of your brain? I love to learn new musical instruments; so far, I have learned to play over 12 instruments. Did you know that learning a musical instrument increases your IQ by five points?

I also love word games, and in my spare time, I play word games such as "*Scrabble*," "*Words With Friends*" and "*Hooked on Words*." These **mental activities keep my mind challenged and motivated.**

Physically

I love to **keep active.** Depending on the season of the year, I love to ride my road-bike or mountain-bike, go cross-country or downhill snow-skiing, play squash or tennis, and either walk or hike. I have a desk job, so I try to do something physical at least five or six times a week.

The other part of the physical equation is having a good diet. Here in North America, it is so easy to overeat ... and I love to eat! But I have learned that being overweight slows me down. So I am learning to be disciplined in my daily intake of food. Currently I use an App on my phone called "*Lose It*," to keep track of my daily caloric intake.

We only get to do life once! Do it with gusto ... go for it! Be prepared, and be one of those who gets to the top of the mountain!

7: WHAT IS YOUR TRUE CALLING?

My first couple of years working in church ministry were great. The church I was born in, *Glad Tidings Church,* had me conduct and arrange music for their 100-voice choir and orchestra. It was a bit intimidating at first – I was only 27 when I started, and many of the choir and orchestra members were significantly older. But leading in the old *Glad Tidings* church building was so much fun! There was such power in the music as we belted out great songs of worship to the Lord: *"Bless the Lord, Who reigns in wisdom and in power"* ... *"Worship the Lord, let's praise His holy Name!"*

I was even blessed to be the Choir Director when the church moved into its new 2,200-seat auditorium. That stage had all the bells and whistles! There was a huge platform in the middle of the stage that went down to the floor below to pick up sets. There were two huge revolving turntables on each side of the stage for rotating sets, and two great curtains for the front and back of the stage. To this day, it is still the best stage I have worked on in church ministry.

Unfortunately, there were also problems: the church could not afford all this grandeur. Significant leadership problems caused the church to not make a good transition to the new building.

The church owed millions of dollars, and the interest was killing it. In the fall of 1984, some of the staff was let go because the church didn't have funds to pay us.

At the time, we were enjoying our 9-month-old son Josh, and Anna was pregnant with our second child (soon-to-be Stephanie). As a family with a child in arms and another on the way, we had some praying to do! I put out my name to other churches, went on *Unemployment Insurance* (*"Thank you, Canadian government"*) and continued to conduct the church choir. We were living in Anna's parents' basement suite, and Anna was back working at the *Royal Bank,* so we were getting by.

A few weeks after being laid off, I was leading the GT Choir on a Sunday evening when I spotted two men in grey business suits sitting in the middle of the congregation – and something told me they had come from another church to "check me out." Indeed they had! They came from *First Assembly* in Calgary ... and in a short time, I was hired to conduct *their* annual *Singing Christmas Tree* and become their new Music Pastor!

That autumn, I was flying back and forth between Vancouver and Calgary, working on two Christmas productions at the same time. Later I turned over the Vancouver production to another leader, and my little family and I moved to Calgary in time to conduct many performances of *"The Singing Christmas Tree."* Busy times!

In the midst of all these changes, God finally showed me what my true calling was. I could lead music groups, and conduct, and write music for choirs and orchestras – but that was not my main calling. When I arrived in Calgary, I turned 30 ... and I began to lead people in Worship for the first time in my life!

That was many years ago, and leading people to set their hearts and worship on God is still one of my greatest pleasures and joys. Leading people to God through Worship has taken me around the world numerous times, and allowed me to minister before hundreds of thousands of people on nearly every continent. I agree with what King David wrote:

The LORD has chosen you to stand in His presence, to minister to Him, and to lead the people in worship.
2 Chronicles 29:11

God knew what He was calling me to do!

8: KEEPING INSPIRED

In life, it is sometimes easy to lose focus, to lose inspiration, to get discouraged. Let me tell you what helps me stay focused, what helps me stay on track; let me tell you what inspires me.

Every morning, I wake early and spend time with my Creator. I spend time with He Who saw me in my mother's womb. I spend time with the One Who spoke the universe into existence. For me, there is no better way to start the day.

I look forward to getting up in the morning and reading the ancient words that are life to billions of people around the world. I love reading the lyrics of the great song-writers of the Bible. I love reading the words and proverbs of the wisest man who ever lived. I love reading the stories of men and women of faith who have gone through struggles and failures, but yet listened to the still, small voice that keeps their hearts on course to God.

Reading God's Word every day keeps me inspired. When I read the *"words in red"* and get to know God's gift sent down to Earth, I am inspired! Do you want to know what God is like? Get to know Jesus!

When I was beginning my journey to knowing Jesus, I read through the Gospels – Matthew through John – five times in a single month. For the last 34 years, I have read through the entire Bible every year. God's Word is life. God's Word is truth. Human "truth" changes with the constant shifting of our culture, but real truth is unchanging.

Words like "*Love your neighbor as yourself*" ... or "*Love the Lord with all your heart, soul, mind, and strength*" ... or "*Go into all the world and preach the Gospel*" – these words give me inspiration. These words keep me on track. These words are **truth.**

Do you want to stay inspired? My suggestion is to take your Bible off the shelf and read it. It will inspire you and recharge your battery. It has changed my life. It can change yours!

9: MY WILD DREAM FROM GOD

In the autumn of 1974, I was 19 years old and had just finished doing a 10-month Christian band tour through nine countries in Asia and the western United States with *Living Sound II*. I was praying about what God wanted me to do next.

Early one Tuesday morning, I had a dream (normally, I never remember my dreams). But in this dream, God was telling me I was supposed to join *Living Sound I*, which had just left for Poland. In my dream, I argued with God, telling Him I had no money. But God gave me the names of three people I should phone, saying they would give me the money.

When I woke from my dream, I talked to the Head Music Director of *Living Sound*, **Larry Dalton**. I told him my dream, and asked what he thought. He said I should phone those three people as the dream had directed, and if the money came in – $1,200, which seemed like a huge amount at the time – then it must be God. I phoned those three people that same morning, and by noon that same day, all the funds came in.

I booked a flight to Chicago to get my Polish visa, and flew out on Thursday. The taxi driver – who, as it turns out, was Polish – was so thrilled to hear my story that he gave me a free ride to the Polish Embassy. On Friday of that same week, I flew into Warsaw, Poland, with a photographer **Scoti Domiej,** and I joined **Don Moen** and *Living Sound I.* They had no idea I was coming because this was before the days of emails and cell phones.

For the next three and a half weeks, we played in huge Catholic cathedrals all over Poland. The cathedrals were packed with thousands wherever we played; one night in particular, 5,000 people were packed so tightly, shoulder to shoulder, that the whole crowd swayed as one.

At every concert, our speaker, **Terry Law,** would give an invitation to people to receive Jesus as their Savior. In those three and a half weeks, over 18,000 people indicated that they wanted to believe in Jesus to forgive their sins and start a relationship with God!

As a byproduct of those concerts, we had lunch with **Cardinal Wojtyla,** who subsequently became Pope John Paul II. The Team was later invited to sing at the Vatican ... but that's another story!

10: GOD USES MENTORS

A fellow Music Pastor, **Blaine Eagle,** recently mentioned he was doing a concert with **Don Moen.** Don and I traveled together for around 18 months in *Living Sound.* He was the Music Director for the Team, and a very hard-working guy.

Don drove our bus, and wrote and arranged most of our music. He played trombone, electric guitar, harmonica, and violin for the band. In fact, Don taught me to play harmonica, which is such a cool instrument. I bought a *Honer Blues Harp,* and asked Don for lessons. To this day, I always bring the harmonica on my hiking trips ... and it's always a big hit when I play it for the Country Music time during the *Calgary Stampede.* There's a recording on one of my CDs of me playing "*The Happy Song*" on harmonica, while touring in Denmark.

Mentors are great. Sometimes they do not even realize they are mentors. Another of my *Living Sound* mentors was the late **Larry Dalton.** He joined our tour in South Africa. I would stand behind him in the band and watch while he did amazing stuff on the piano. When he needed a music copyist, I volunteered – not only because I was hungry to learn how to write music and orchestrations – but because it is great to learn from the best.

Larry was an incredible pianist. I remember attending a huge Music Pastors' Conference in San Diego (*Music California*) and seeing Larry play as a guest soloist. One of his favorite crowd-pleasers was to take requests from the audience – anything from movie themes, TV themes, hymns, songs, anything! (such as anything from "*Theme from the Flintstones*" to "*What a Friend We Have in Jesus*") – and he would make a 7- to 10-minute medley that would leave the audience cheering, standing on their feet! He was amazing.

I'm thankful for all the amazing mentors in my life:

- **Doug Moody,** my first piano teacher, and church choir and Big Band director
- **Mrs. Robinson,** my high school Band teacher
- **Glen Geary,** my incredible piano teacher from the *University of British Columbia* (I was scared to go into a lesson with him without having first practiced three hours per day)
- **Dan Burr,** the leader of the first music group I was in at *Glad Tidings*: **New Dimensions and Liberty Brass**
- **Jim Gilbert,** my *Living Sound* Director on the Asian Tour (I remember him singing lead while

playing a pump organ in a Korean garment factory; I also remember him writing "*I Love You With the Love of the Lord*")

- **Don Moen,** my *Living Sound* Music Director in Europe and South Africa
- **Larry Dalton,** the head Music Director of *Living Sound.*

Such great musicians and inspiring people to learn from and work with!

11: LEARNING ABOUT SURRENDER

In the autumn of 1973, I was in the second year of my Bachelor of Music studies at the University of British Columbia, but frankly I wasn't doing well. I was struggling with the demands of the long practice times and the studies, and I decided to quit university. In reality, I was losing my focus and purpose for studying Music.

I wasn't sure what I would do next, so I prayed and fasted, and then started to apply for jobs that would work with my Math skills. I applied for banking, accounting, brokerage, and a host of other jobs ... and much to my surprise, a number of places started offering me jobs. But I never started any of the jobs because another, better one, would quickly come along.

A few weeks later, on a Wednesday night in November, the Christian music group *Living Sound* played at my church. That night, when **Terry Law** preached, I was challenged to surrender my whole life to God. God broke down my fears and reluctance to follow Him wholeheartedly, and I responded to the message that night.

You have to understand that initially I was afraid of giving my whole life to God. I had an

aunt who spent most of her single life in Africa ...
and I didn't want to be a single missionary (the
song, "*Lord, Please Don't Send Me to Africa*," comes to
mind). But **when God speaks to you, suddenly
your fears disappear.** I have found that God
usually asks me to come to a place of surrendering
my own will and desires, before He begins to use
me in new endeavors.

On Thursday, after hearing Terry Law's
sermon, I auditioned for *Living Sound*, and one day
later, they asked if I would join their Team Two in
Seattle on Monday. I would need a passport and
$1,300 to help pay my airfare for five months of
traveling in Asia. I didn't have a passport or
$1,300, but God made a way that weekend; by
Monday, I had the passport and the finances in
place.

For the next two and a half years, I traveled
with *Living Sound* throughout Asia, North
America, Europe, Poland, South Africa, and Israel.
We saw over 100,000 people come to the Lord, all
over the world. I also worked with some of the
top ministries of that time, and learned hands-on
ministry in real-life situations. I never attended
Bible School, but I couldn't have asked for a better
introduction to full-time ministry. When I
finished that tour with *Living Sound* in 1976, I had
regained my passion and purpose for Music, and

went back and finished my Music degree in preparation for what God would do next.

November 2013 marked 40 years since I went into full-time ministry. I have now traveled to more than 60 countries and seen over 250,000 people make the decision for the Lord, overseas and at home in Canada. I have never regretted following God to the corners of the Earth or working in the local church.

Surrendering to God and following Him with your whole heart is exciting.

12: GOD LOVES ME EVEN WHEN I DO DUMB THINGS

When we are young, we don't always think things through ... and sometimes we do dumb stuff. Let me give you an example.

When I was 19, I was traveling with *Living Sound* in England. One day we had the day off, so a number of us went shopping in London. Somehow, I was talked into trying on an Afro wig. Who knows why I did it, but I ended up buying that Afro wig. Weird, yes, I know. But sometimes we do dumb stuff. In my defense, Afros were popular back then.

Soon after, we decided to persuade as many of our band members as possible to wear their hair in Afro styles, for a concert at a church. That night, there were seven of us in Afros. Who knows why? It just sounded like a fun thing to do.

Our band was often billeted at peoples' homes, and on this particular night, I was billeted with three other guys from our band at the pastor's home. Normally, we would stay just one night, but because of a gap in our tour, we stayed three nights.

When we arrived at the pastor's home after the concert, I was embarrassed to let our hosts know I had been wearing a wig ... so I kept it on for the whole three days. If you've ever worn a wig, you know it can get really itchy. Finally on the last morning, I couldn't take it any longer. I showered, then blow-dried my own hair to its typical bone-straight. When I went down for breakfast, the pastor's family was shocked. "How did you get your hair so straight?" they asked.

Again, I was too embarrassed to admit I had been wearing a wig, so I just responded, "I just blow-dried it and it came out straight." Dumb answer, I know! But in my defense, I was young ... and dumb.

I recently heard **John Maxwell** speak at a Leadership symposium. He started by telling of the dumb things he's done. He told about getting the gift of a beautiful handgun (even though he's not a big gun-fan). Someone asked if he knew how to load it. Before John knew it, the gun was loaded ... then he put it in his briefcase, and forgot about it. He forgot about it until he was going through Security at an American airport. As his bag was going through screening, John pointed at the x-ray machine and said, "Oh! There's a loaded gun in there!" As you can imagine, John Maxwell spent more than a few hours in Security, explaining his way out of that dumb mistake.

His story reminded me of another dumb thing I did while on tour. When I was 19, I was in a Christian band playing in Poland. Most of our concerts were in large Catholic cathedrals, but one evening we found ourselves playing at a Polish night club. After we finished playing, the band spread out in the club and struck up conversations with different patrons, talking about Jesus.

I ended up at a table with six people who were celebrating a birthday. They had smuggled in Polish vodka, and as we talked, they kept filling up my glass. I grew up in a family who never drank alcohol. At the end of the evening, when I got up to leave, suddenly I found the whole room spinning. I carefully hung onto chairs as I headed for our bus.

Talk about dumb! When Jesus said, "*Eat whatever is set before you*" (see Luke 10:8), I'm sure He wasn't talking about Polish vodka! Fortunately, we all can learn from our mistakes ... and I never did that again.

I appreciate God's love for me, even when I do dumb things. It is like when my grandson accidentally spills milk at our house. Anna and I love him so much that we quickly clean up after him and don't make a big fuss. His mistakes do not change our love for him in the slightest. And God's love for me is even greater than that!

13: THE DANGEROUS BIRTHDAY

My twentieth birthday was very memorable. I was traveling with *Living Sound* in Rhodesia (now Zimbabwe). We had the day off, and we were spending it on a beautiful estate, with a gorgeous house, rolling lawns and great amenities.

The house had a sauna, so I thought I would try it out. I hadn't spent more than 10 minutes in the sauna when suddenly the room was filled with the other guys in the band. They grabbed me, carried me out onto the lawn, and while some of the guys sat on me, a girl from the band shaved my right leg.

You need to understand that I have very hairy legs. This was in December, which is the middle of summer in Africa. I always wear shorts in the summer. Now I was sporting one very hairy leg and one clean-shaven leg – not a great "look."

Why would this happen? In our band, it was very "dangerous" to have a birthday while on tour. On our trip to Africa on a cruise ship, my buddy Greg had been grabbed from his bunk bed early one morning. He was fast asleep – then eight of the guys surprised him by throwing him into the ship's pool. It was retaliation for interfering with us getting his girlfriend on *her* birthday. Sure, we were serious about our ministry around the world, but we also had to have some opportunities to harmlessly blow off steam.

The best story, which is sort of legendary, was when our fearless leader **Terry Law** had his birthday. Terry was one of the worst for pulling birthday pranks; naturally, as his birthday approached, he was quite wary of what could happen to him. Terry kept looking over his shoulder the whole day, wondering when "it" (the birthday prank) would happen.

Dinner came, just before our evening concert, and still nothing had happened. Unbeknown to Terry, the girls on the team had prepared a special birthday cake for him. They made a chocolate cake with one very special piece: they had laced Terry's portion with a couple of chocolate-flavored *Ex-Lax* (a very strong laxative) tablets mixed into the icing. When they served the birthday cake just before the service, Terry got his "special" piece of cake. He had no idea what was happening.

The team held their concert that night, and as usual, Terry came up to preach. As he was preaching his 7-point sermon, the *Ex-Lax* kicked in around his third point. The team could see his obvious discomfort as he cut his 40-minute sermon to 20-minutes and quickly passed it off to another team-member to close.

Apparently Terry spent the rest of the night staying very close to the bathroom. So, being in music ministry on the road could be very dangerous if you were having your birthday in our band.

14: MY FAVORITE MUSIC GIGS, SO FAR

From my travels around the world, here are 12 musical highlights (thus far). I thank God for opening these doors for me to do these very special gigs!

Charles Ndifon's Meetings
Copenhagen, Denmark

In that week of meetings, we saw more 15,000 people raise their hands to know Jesus. For me, this started a 7-year around-the-world journey of seeing healings, miracles and tens of thousands of people accepting Jesus.

Living Sound Poland Meetings
Warsaw to Krakow, Poland

In those three-and-a-half weeks of meetings in huge Catholic cathedrals all over Poland, we saw over 18,000 people accept Jesus. On this trip we met the man who would later become Pope John Paul II, and that led to the team playing at the Vatican a few years later.

Conference on the Holy Spirit
Jerusalem and Tel Aviv, Israel

This was my first time visiting Israel. We worked with one of the most well-known healing ministers of that day: **Kathryn Kuhlman.** We also did the music for her meetings in both Jerusalem and Tel Aviv. To top it off, we took sightseeing tours around Israel, which is one of life's great experiences. Meeting Miss Kuhlman, playing at the meetings, then touring around Israel were all incredible experiences.

Billy Graham Crusade
Vancouver, British Columbia, Canada

I was extremely blessed to be the Chairman of Music for the *Billy Graham Crusade* in Vancouver. On the closing night, there were over 65,000 people in *B.C. Place Stadium,* and more than 3,000 people responded to the invitation. I learned so much working with this highly-organized, extremely-dedicated team of men and women.

Calgary Stampede
Calgary, Alberta, Canada

I was asked to be the Musical Arranger and Conductor for a large production number of "*O Canada*" for the nightly *Calgary Stampede*

"*Chuckwagon Races and Grandstand Show.*" The *Calgary Stampede* is called the "greatest outdoor show on Earth." For those who do not know the Canadian National Anthem "*O Canada,*" it is a prayer for God to "*keep our land glorious and free.*"

Of the three years I conducted this event, my favorite was on the 100th Anniversary of the *Stampede.* We put together a 200-voice choir and a top-notch band to perform before 300,000 people that year.

Christian Bookseller's Convention
Anaheim, California, U.S.A.

Growing up, my "musical hero" was Grammy Award-winning writer and singer **Andraé Crouch.** During this Convention, the band I was playing with (*Living Sound*) performed before 12,000 people, and I was also asked to play in Andraé's band on a couple of numbers. That was so cool – I got to play with my musical hero!

Alvin Slaughter Concert
Christian Life Assembly, Langley, B.C., Canada

One awesome June evening at *Christian Life Assembly,* with the church packed with around 1,600 people, I conducted the choir and orchestra, and our guest soloist Alvin Slaughter just rocked the place. Alvin was the former assistant director of the *Brooklyn Tabernacle Choir,* and an incredible lead soloist. He is one of the best singers I have ever worked with. It was a very special musical evening.

Vivien Hibbert
International Worship Institute, Dallas, Texas

For several years, I was the Daytime Music Director for the *International Worship Institute* in Dallas, and one morning I played with **Vivien Hibbert.** I really did not know what to expect, but God came down in a very tangible way that morning.

Musically speaking, it was very basic. Vivien led a few worship songs and played a very mellow large recorder-type of instrument. I directed a small band and accompanied her on keyboard and flute. God came down in such a heavy way that the whole place was on the floor kneeling before the Lord in reverence. The presence of God was amazing!

Promise Keepers Meetings
Vancouver

One year I was asked to be the Music Director for the *Promise Keepers* meetings in Vancouver. We put together a great team of some of the top Christian musicians from around the area, and we led Worship for thousands of men that whole weekend. I can still picture the men worshipping God with their whole hearts. What a great experience and honor.

Yoido Full Gospel Church with Dr. Paul Yonggi Cho, Sr.
Seoul, South Korea

On our 5-month Asian Tour, one of the first places the *Living Sound Asian Team* played was at the (then) largest church in the world. We played several Sunday morning services at *Yoido Full Gospel Church*, in Seoul, South Korea, and even had dinner with Dr. Paul Yonggi Cho, Sr. I think the church was around 70,000 members then, and it has now grown to close to 1,000,000. I was totally impressed by the passion of those South Korean Christians.

Nicky Cruz Meetings
Capetown to Durban, South Africa

Nicky Cruz was a former New York gang leader turned evangelist. He became well-known through the book "*The Cross and the Switchblade,*" written by David Wilkerson. Nicky spoke at a number of meetings all over South Africa, and our band *Living Sound* was asked to do the music for the meetings. In those great outdoor venues, we saw a great response to the message to know Jesus.

Waikiki Beach Chaplaincy
Honolulu, Hawaii

This was one of the last concerts of our *Living Sound's* Asian Tour, and we could not have asked for a more beautiful setting to worship through music. Wearing shorts and tee-shirts, we played on Waikiki Beach, in front of the *Hilton Hawaiian* Rainbow Towers. We also played at *Fort DeRussy,* just a few blocks further down the beach. Both of those venues were some of the most relaxed and beautiful places I ever played. A cool experience!

15: HANGING OUT WITH BILLY GRAHAM

Throughout my life, I have been blessed to work with – and learn from – great men and women of God. One of my first mentors was **Doug Moody.** Doug was the Music Pastor at *Glad Tidings,* the church where I grew up. He was a master musician, and I was blessed to have taken piano lessons from him for many years. I recall Doug writing Big Band charts and other orchestrations for his albums and recordings. Doug was a big inspiration to me, my first musical mentor. When Doug stepped down from conducting *Glad Tidings'* 120-voice choir and orchestra, I was blessed (and more than a bit intimidated) to follow as the next conductor and arranger. Talk about "big shoes to fill"!

When *The Billy Graham Crusade* came to Vancouver in 1984, I was honored to become the Chairman of Music for the Crusade. Frankly, I didn't deserve that honor. The Crusade Team routinely asked the Choir Director with the biggest choir in town to be the Chairman — and I just happened to have inherited Doug's great choir. He deserved the honor; I was just a fortunate substitute.

One evening before the Crusade, Anna and I had dinner with **Billy Graham** and the Crusade

Team. Wow! We sat at a table with **George Beverly Shea** – double wow! I was all of 29 years old. What an undeserved honor. They were great people and incredible world-changers, faithful servants of God. What a great team they had! I was so blessed to spend that week with them at the Crusade.

Another special person I met and worked with was **Kathryn Kuhlman.** Kathryn had an amazing healing ministry which touched people around the world. In 1975, our *Living Sound* Team was asked to provide music for her meetings in Jerusalem and Tel Aviv, Israel. She came to our pre-service prayer meetings. She was so friendly and gracious; she reminded me of my Grandma Cole. Ms. Kuhlman was 68 years old at the time, and – as it turned out – this was her last public meeting before she passed away the following February.

To be able to have met and worked with such amazing people was such a privilege. They have set the bar so high. Their passion and faithfulness to do the work of God, and preach the Good News of Jesus, is outstanding.

16: LEARNING TO TRUST GOD

Have you ever gone through a major transition in your life and wondered what God was doing? In 2008, I was going through one of those transitions. I had just left the staff at a church ... and I didn't have any new plans. That's always a bit scary! There are always bills to pay, a family to support, and a life to live.

It is amazing how God directs my paths and supplies my needs. That summer, the first surprise was to be asked by **Linda Bakken** of the *Stampede Chuckwagon Committee* to do a big special production number of "*O Canada*" (the national anthem) for the *Calgary Stampede,* which is billed as "the greatest outdoor show on Earth." Hundreds of thousands of people come to Calgary, Alberta, from all over the world to enjoy the Rodeo, the Chuckwagon Races, and the Grandstand shows – ten days of awesome outdoor shows. Calgary turns into a fun western town for the full Stampede.

For the production number, I helped put together a marching band and brass section, with guest soloist **Christine Chester.** I did my best "David Foster" imitation: playing a grand piano and conducting the musicians. Every night we played for crowds of 25,000 to 30,000 people. For those not familiar with the Canadian anthem, it is a prayer for God to bless our country. How cool is that! During those ten days, I got to conduct a musical prayer in front of around 270,000 people for "*my home and native land*": the great country of Canada. What a great gig!

The other door the Lord opened that summer was writing for a big musical event in Toronto, Ontario. A buddy of mine, **Steve Munshaw,** was asked to produce an event called "*Heaven's Rehearsal.*" Steve asked me to be the Musical Director for the event, but because of logistical problems and the costs of working on an event that far away, I ended up writing all the charts and orchestrations for the musical and Worship extravaganza. For the better part of two months, I sat in my office and wrote full vocal and orchestra parts for a myriad of different Worship songs.

There were great upbeat Gospel tunes, Gaither-style quartet pieces, major choir pieces, and a host of great Worship tunes ... with soloists, singers, choir, and a 40-piece orchestra. Although I was not able to attend the weekend in Toronto, I saw the great video footage. Steve Munshaw, the band, the choir, the dancers, all did an awesome job. I was very proud to have been part of that project.

Those two projects covered my expenses, and kept me very busy until God called me to work at *Eastside City Church* in Calgary, where I led Worship for almost six years. God knows what you need, and when you need it.

The longer I walk with God, the more I trust Him.

17: THE POWER IN OF A GREAT TEAM

It has always amazed me how much we can accomplish when we work with a team. For the first dozen years I was in church ministry, huge Christmas, Easter and Canada Day productions were a large part of my responsibilities.

At *Christian Life Assembly* in Langley, B.C., it took a large team to help organize and pull off those productions. I used to write the scripts, compile the songs and orchestrations, and start music rehearsals. **Faith Bateman** would assemble a team, audition the actors, and start drama rehearsals. **Ron Low** would begin building sets, and gather a team of people to do all the building and backstage work. **Glen Beitel** would work on special effects and organizing the live animals. **Paulette Hawkings** would work on costume design, and gather a team of seamstresses who made the costumes. **Ann Zauner** would compile the team of make-up artists. There was also **Bob Long** and his sound team, and another team for the lighting crew. And I can't forget the head usher and his team, and the group who worked on advertising. There were lots of people involved, lots of leaders, lots of teamwork.

Writers ... orchestrators ... musicians ... soloists ... choir ... children's choir ... actors ... make-up team ... costumes ... lighting ... sound ... set builders ... special effects people ... flying team ... prayer team ... advertising ... ushers ... clean-up crew ... art ... graphics ... and the list goes on! When the church works together as a team, when everyone uses their gifts and talents, it is amazing what can be accomplished.

I am thankful for those days! It took a lot of planning and hard work, but it was great to see the church filled night after night. It was awesome to see people respond to the Good News of Jesus when **Pastor Brent Cantelon** gave the invitation at the end. It was fun to see the camaraderie and friendships that grew as that large team of very talented people worked together for one common purpose.

There is great power in Christian community and teamwork!

Afterwords

Faith Bateman (director): *They were wonderful days, albeit super-busy. Our team's families were all involved, our kids played together and ate together, and many grew up on the stage ... and learned the art of servanthood working backstage. We also must not forget* *the dedicated prayer warriors who would roam the auditorium while we rehearsed and worked on sets, who would be in the Prayer Room during performances. I will always be grateful to have been part of it for almost 15 years.*

Brent Sheppard (actor; playing Jesus and other parts): *The "Acrobatic Jesus" was the best; made the local news. I remember the choir below, singing, arms raised in worship ... then they saw "Acrobatic Jesus" rotate out and over them, their eyes wide as He was about to do a dive or a flip, and the choir's arms went from "Worship mode" to "catch Him!" Jesus did a full rotation, came around perfectly, and smiling because He was "truly still alive" ... then, up in "Heaven," there was Ron Low waiting to pull me in, big grin on his face. To this day I think Ron put that harness on wrong! Great fun.*

Note from Mark: *Brent Sheppard played the part of Jesus that Easter. During the Ascension scene, as he was raised 40 feet in the air by our harness system, something went wrong and he started to spin end-over-end! Hilarious, but totally inappropriate.*

Lisa Kramer (cast and choir member): *Such a big fun part of my growing up! So many hours spent at the church; we kids loved every minute of it. Great memories!*

Sylvia Butler: *Those were awesome times of ministry! The message is the same but the way it is presented can* change. Faith Bateman is correct about the prayer. Even after all the hours of preparation done so willingly, we all needed God's anointing to touch hearts to hear the message. I well remember my tears being very real over the Easter weekend productions, as I felt the part. Our children grew up being involved along with us. Precious times indeed, because I was fortunate to talk with folks afterward who were changed by what they saw and heard. That's why we all gave so much of our time.

18: GREAT, LIFE-CHANGING BOOKS

Reading has always been a big part of my life. When I was a kid, I read over 100 *Hardy Boys* books that were handed down to me by a friend. Later, when I was traveling in a band, I was introduced to some great Christian classics through Terry Law, the pastor who traveled with us.

In university, I was a Music major and an English minor, and read many of the classic English novels and the works of Shakespeare. I love reading! I have read through the Bible – itself a collection of 66 books – over 30 times, in most of the major translations.

Some books are good entertainment for the moment, and some books stick with you throughout your life. Here is my top list of books that have influenced or remained with me to this day.

• *Knowing God* by **J.I. Packer.** This is a Christian classic. Packer challenged me to really set my heart on knowing God. In this great book, he really reveals the joy and wonder of knowing the Creator.

- *The Living Bible,* a paraphrase by **Kenneth N. Taylor.** This is the first version of the Bible that I ever read cover to cover. I love its ease of reading. Taylor wrote this paraphrase so his kids could understand the Bible.

- *The Hobbit* and *The Lord of the Rings Trilogy* by **J.R. Tolkien.** The battle between good and evil, and the adventurous and brave spirits of Bilbo Baggins and his nephew Frodo are inspiring. These four books also translated into great movies.

- *The Screwtape Letters* by **C.S. Lewis.** Professor Lewis uses this classic and satirical book of a conversation between demons, to teach us about the tricks of the devil.

- *Experiencing God* by **Henry T. Blackaby.** Great insight into how God works in the hearts of people who seek Him. It was so good to recognize God's own workings in my life through this book.

- *Spiritual Authority* by **Watchman Nee.** My first glimpse of how God sets up authority in His Kingdom.

- *The Pursuit of God* by **A.W. Tozer.** I love Tozer's passion for God. It inspires me.

- *The New International Version Bible.* This is the second translation of the Bible that I read through. A great translation.

- *The Secret Kingdom* by **Pat Robertson.** The parables of Jesus were explained to me in such real terms.

- *The Testament* by **John Grisham.** I have read all of Grisham's novels, and his description of a personal conversion in this entertaining novel is inspiring.

- *Exploring Worship* by **Bob Sorge.** I have worked with Bob on numerous occasions, and his practical advice on church worship is foundational.

- *In His Steps* by **Charles M. Sheldon.** A short Christian novel that has still got me asking, *"What would Jesus do?"*

- *Secrets of the Secret Place* by **Bob Sorge.** Getting to know God begins in our private times with God. Bob's insight into seeking God rang true in my heart.

- *Just As I Am* by **Billy Graham.** I was honored to work with Dr. Graham, and I was fascinated to read the behind-the-scenes of his life and ministry around the world.

- *Chronicles of Narnia* by **C.S. Lewis.** I read this book series one summer when I was teaching in Taiwan. The books captivated and entertained me. I usually read one of these seven short books at a single sitting.

- *Good to Great* and *Social Sectors* by **Jim Collins.** I love Jim's style of writing, and his insight into the business world. These principles also translate well into the non-profit world.

- *Axiom* by **Bill Hybels.** I visited Pastor Hybel's church in Chicago, and I love his wisdom and insight into church culture and leadership.

- *The 7 Habits of Highly Effective People* by **Steven R. Covey.** This book helped me examine my life and improve it. I still go back to refer to this book as source material.

- *The New Living Translation Bible.* This is the translation of the Bible that I currently love reading. It is the translation I recommend to people looking to read God's Word.

19: GOD KNEW MY NEEDS BEFORE I DID

In 1998, I was the Music Director for *Canada Arise,* a Worship Conference in Vancouver. This was an annual Worship Conference held in *Glad Tidings Church,* where I was the Music Pastor. During the Conference, a number of people asked me for copies of the charts (brass, vocals, rhythm) which I created for my own Worship band and the various guest Worship leaders who came. **Ryan Dahl** was a young Worship Pastor who was also looking for a business to start; he asked me for charts. Later, Ryan asked if he could sell my charts. I was happy to let him sell them, but only if he got all the legal permissions and did the business part. I was only interested in writing Music.

At first, Ryan would fax the music to other Worship leaders, but around that time the idea of an Internet business was just taking off. Very soon after, Ryan started *PraiseCharts.com.* He would take my charts, scan them into .pdf files and sell them via the Internet through an ever-growing network of Worship leaders. Very quickly, *PraiseCharts* grew into a full-fledged business, with salaries and royalties for Ryan, myself and other employees.

In the autumn of 1999, the Lord indicated to me that I should resign from my position at *Glad Tidings*. I assumed I would be working full-time writing music for *PraiseCharts*. It was difficult for me to think about not leading Worship in a church, but I couldn't shake the idea that I was supposed to resign by February 2000; so I put in my resignation.

Leaving a church is always a hard thing to do. I had built relationships with all the musicians. In my case, this was even harder because I had grown up in *Glad Tidings,* and many of the Worship band members had been my friends since our teens. We had also recorded three original Worship CDs – *"To You, Lord"* ... *"God Is My Rock"* ... and *"Move In This City"* – while I was on staff. But when God begins to move you – even if all the details don't make immediate sense – I've learned to follow.

Through another series of events, I ended up leaving *Glad Tidings* a few months early. And in January 2000, I was at home thinking, *"What have I done? I love leading congregations in Worship! What am I doing at home just writing music?"* I have to admit I was not a happy camper! I was having serious doubts about what was happening.

Then out of nowhere, I received a phone call from an evangelist who had ministered at *Glad Tidings* a few times. **Charles Ndifon** asked if I would fly to Copenhagen in February, and lead Worship for a week of meetings he was doing there. I accepted his invitation, and the next month I was on a flight to Denmark. What happened next was remarkable!

That week of meetings are the most incredible I have ever experienced! We had meetings twice a day, and every day thousands of people indicated they wanted to know more about Jesus. At the end of the week, Charles asked if I wanted more; I, of course, could hardly wait.

For the next six years, I was boarding an airplane every other week to join Charles and lead worship in countries like Sweden ... Norway ... Denmark ... Holland ... England ... Germany ... Finland ... Switzerland ... Austria ... Iceland ... Australia ... the United States of America ... Canada ... Nigeria ... Zimbabwe ... and Uganda. We saw thousands of people from all over the world come to faith in Jesus, and many hundreds healed. In Denmark alone, over 75,000 people came to the Lord.

Between meetings, when I was at home, I would write music for *PraiseCharts*. This source –

and what I received from selling my three original Worship CDs from *Glad Tidings* – were my main income. I received honorariums from Charles' meetings but they would never have been enough to support my family at home, in Langley.

God already knew His plans for me to travel around the world, leading Worship. He knew the finances I needed even before I knew. God had set-up my *PraiseCharts* income, and He had also led me to records those *Glad Tidings* worship CDs.

God knew my needs before I did.

20: **GOD** *CAN* **TOUCH A NATION**

In February 2000, I left home for a week to lead Worship for Charles Ndifon, in Copenhagen, Denmark, at *Kiren i Kulturcenteret (CPH Christian Center)*.

Charles had been in Denmark in 1999, and had ministered to a small college group in the Danish town of Ringkobing. At that same time, a Danish TV show was doing a series on "spiritualism," and when they heard that someone with a healing ministry was coming to Ringkobing, they wanted to do a test. They found a man named Roger, who had been in an accident which had messed up his vision. Then they filmed as they took Roger to a doctor and got an official report on him.

The TV show then took Roger to Charles' meetings, and asked him to pray for him. Charles told them to have Roger (who wasn't a Christian) sit in the meeting, and let God do what He would.

During the meeting, Roger received Jesus as his Savior. Later in the meeting, when Charles was praying a general prayer for healing, Roger was miraculously healed, his vision totally restored! All of this was captured by the TV crew. From this, a TV show was produced that showed a *bona fide* miracle that was documented by a doctor and filmed by a secular TV crew. Wow!

Before we arrived in Copenhagen in 2000, this TV show had been broadcast to the entire nation of Denmark. The Danish people realized that God still heals people.

We had two meetings per day during that first week in Copenhagen. I vividly remember that first meeting: the church was filled to overflow with around 1,800 people ... and when the invitation to receive Jesus Christ in their lives was given, 80% of the people in the room put up their hands. I had never seen anything like that in my life. By the end of the week, over 15,000 people indicated they wanted to know Jesus. Double wow!!

When we left Denmark at the end of the week, *Kiren i Kulturcenteret* (the local church) was in a bit of panic because over 4,000 people had signed up for their "*Alpha Program*" (a twelve-week dinner program introducing, or discipling, people into Christianity) – and they had no idea how they would handle that many people. (That's a great problem to have!)

After that, we were invited to come to Denmark many times each year, for several years.

The secular press estimated over 75,000 people made decisions for Jesus in the next few years. (I believe there were many more.)

If you would like to read more about this amazing time, check out the book "*The God of Miracles: A Danish Journalist Examines Healings in the Ministry of Charles Ndifon* " by Henri Nissen (see more in **Recommendations**, at the back of this book). It is a book on many of the miracles we saw during those extraordinary times. I was blessed to have proofread it before it was published. The stories are amazing and true!

God can touch a nation!

21: THE BEST ADVENTURE

I love adventure! I have been parachuting ... bungee jumping ... barefoot water-skiing ... caving ... mountain climbing ... scuba diving ... high-speed snow-skiing ... backpacking in Alaska ... extreme mountain biking ... white water rafting ... back-country, cross-country snow-skiing in avalanche country ... cliff diving ... and a host of other extreme adventures. I love a challenge. I love getting my adrenalin going!

For all the amazing experiences I have had in my life, following God with total abandon has been my greatest adventure. God has always had great surprises and adventures for me. Like that summer God opened the opportunity for me to travel around the world.

My first stop was with my band in Uganda and Kenya. We had an awesome time. We did numerous great concerts in Kampala, Uganda, and then headed to Nairobi, Kenya, to work with a large African choir. One very memorable evening, there were over 5,000 people packed into a church. We had two hours of dancing, singing and praising God. A room full of Africans praising God is the best crowd in the world with whom to share a night of music. The place rocked!

After that, went went "on safari" to the *Masai Mara Game Reserve* in Kenya. Masai Mara is probably the premier game reserve in all of Africa. My young family joined me at this point. Together we saw elephants, lions, cheetahs, leopards, rhinos, hippos, and a host of other great African wildlife in their natural habitat. It was the trip of a life-time. But it did not end there.

My next stop on this God-adventure was India. I was named after a famous missionary: **Mark Buntain,** from Calcutta, India. By the time I arrived, Mark had passed away, but his widow Huldah was still carrying on his work. I contacted her and told her I would love to visit their work. She replied, "Your grandmother used to teach me Sunday School [at *Glad Tidings*]. Please come as my guest and stay in my home." Wow!

I spent two glorious days visiting and working with *Calcutta Mercy Ministries'* 5,000 employees. They run schools, churches, feeding programs, and a hospital there in northern India. What an inspiring visit. To this day, I marvel at the impact which one couple, Mark and Hulda Buntain – totally dedicated to God – can have!

When I finished my short stay in India, I headed off to Taiwan, to work on three Worship CDs that I was producing in Mandarin Chinese.

For a solid week, I recorded all the Chinese vocals to add to the instrumental tracks I had already recorded in Canada. The recordings would later be smuggled into Red China for distribution to the underground church. What a totally cool and amazing experience! God-adventures are the best.

I do not know what God has planned for your life, but frankly, I cannot think of anyone better to trust! I have trusted God to direct my paths since I was a teenager, and it has been an amazing journey.

Once more, let me share my life's verse with you:

Trust in the LORD with all your heart, and don't lean on your own understanding. In all your ways, acknowledge Him, and He will direct your paths.
Proverbs 3:5-6

Honestly, God is the best Adventure Guide I know!

Part Two: TECHNIQUE

Over the past 40 years, I have taught Music and
Worship seminars in many different corners of
our beautiful planet. It's been fun to share my
hard-earned experience and lessons with eager
students from a multitude of cultures and ethnic
backgrounds. Here are some of the things I have
learned along the way.

22: IT IS A PRIVILEGE TO LEAD WORSHIP

One of the greatest privileges I have is leading people to God through Worship. I spent ten years traveling around the world leading Worship, but there is something quite special about working with a local team of musicians and your own local congregation on a weekly basis.

I grew up in a great worshipping church. As a kid in the congregation, I loved singing with the musicians and singers who called our church "home." I loved to sing to the One Who had forgiven all my sins. I loved to clap my hands and raise them in abandon to the Lord. When I was old enough, I started playing in our church band. At first that was a bit intimidating, but as I got better, it became fun.

Worshipping God on the piano was also a very private practice I did in the basement of my home. When I was feeling down, I would sit and play for hours. I loved playing to the Lord. I still love sensing His presence as I spend time playing before Him.

As a musician, the Bible character David (harp-player and warrior) is with whom I most identify. I can relate to the hours he spent playing his music before the Lord. I understand him organizing musicians for Worship. I also appreciate his love of the outdoors and animals, and his sense of adventure. I too love to climb mountains and hike in the wilderness.

I also can relate to David's weaknesses. I really appreciate how God gives us all the warts and failures of the great men and women of the Bible – it makes them so human and believable. The Bible doesn't put them on some kind of super-human pedestal. I love David's repentant heart. When confronted with one of his mistakes, he wrote: *"Create in me a clean heart. ... Cast me not away from Your presence, O LORD"* (Psalm 51). When I have made my own mistakes, David's words rang very true for me.

To be able to train a group of young musicians to become passionate worshippers is a challenge – a challenge that I love. To see them grow up in the Lord, developing their talents and leadership abilities, and then going on to lead their own congregations is an amazing, fulfilling thing.

I have been leading Worship for almost thirty years. For me, it never gets old. To see God's faithfulness, to sing great new songs of Worship, to lead people to encounter the living God on a weekly basis ... priceless! I love what the Bible says:

The LORD has chosen you to stand in His presence, to minister to Him, and to lead the people in worship.

1 Chronicles 29:11; NLT

It is a privilege to lead worship!

23: ATTITUDE IS EVERYTHING

I have been leading congregations and other gatherings in Worship for over 25 years. In my busiest seasons, I have led Worship up to 14 times in a single week.

I did not always feel like it. Sometimes I just wanted to stay home and relax. But I have come to learn that having a proper attitude in life and in worship is so important! Jesus said:

God is looking for true worshippers who will worship Him in spirit and in truth.

John 4:24

God doesn't like fake! God wants our hearts to be true before Him. The Bible says:

*The eyes of the LORD search the whole Earth in order to strengthen those whose hearts are **fully** committed to Him.*

2 Chronicles 16:9; emphasis added

Did you catch that word "*fully*"? I want to be one of those "*true worshippers*" who is *fully* engaged. I want to have a proper attitude when I worship God.

Here are a number of the attitudes of Worship I have discovered in the Bible.

Thankfulness

I love it when my kids and grandkids express their thankfulness for a gift I have given them or something I have done for them. I love it when they don't take those things for granted.

God is the same. He wants us to have thankful hearts when we come to worship Him. Over and over in the Bible, we read the words: *"Give thanks to God"* or *"Giving thanks always"* or *"Be thankful"* or *"Thanks be to God"* or *"With thanksgiving."*

Having a grateful heart is huge! When we realize the depths and heights of His love, and the great gift of His Son Jesus, how can we be anything but thankful?

Honesty

When I read through the Psalms, I am sometimes shocked at the honesty of the writers! We can really tell when they are going through struggles: their humanness shows through.

God is not surprised at the difficulties we go through. He knows when we have been treated unfairly, knows when we have been hurt. Frankly, we are never going to shock Him.

Some of the best song lyrics come from the deepest sorrows and tragedies. Think of the great hymn, "*It Is Well With My Soul*":

When peace, like a river, attendeth my way
When sorrows like sea billows roll
Whatever my lot, Thou hast taught me to say
"It is well, it is well, with my soul"

It is well with my soul
It is well, it is well with my soul

Though Satan should buffet, though trials should come
Let this blessed assurance control
That Christ hath regarded my helpless estate
And hath shed His own blood for my soul.

Those lyrics were born out of a ship collision at sea that took the lives of Horatio Spafford's four daughters. When we begin to understand the depths of the writer's sorrow, then the faith behind the lyrics begins to shine like a beacon of hope.

Reverence

I grew up on the West Coast of Canada, and I love informality. But when we come before the King of Kings, sometimes we need to remember to come with reverence.

The writer of the book of Hebrews put it this way:

Therefore, since we are receiving a Kingdom that cannot be shaken, let us be thankful, and so worship God acceptably with reverence and awe.
Hebrews 12:28

Sometimes, in our need for informality, we forget Who God is. If we really understand Who God is, then reverence and awe will naturally be a part of our attitudes.

Faith

I want my Worship to be pleasing to God:

It is impossible to please God without faith. Anyone who wants to come to Him, must believe that He exists and that He rewards those who sincerely seek Him.
Hebrews 11:6

When I lift my hands in worship and sing to God, I have faith that He is there. I have never seen God, but frequently I sense His presence. But even if I never sense that He is close, God is pleased when I seek Him. He is pleased when we have the faith to worship Him, no matter what our feelings are.

Humility

James, the half-brother of Jesus, said:

God opposed the proud, but shows favor to the humble.

James 4:6

Frankly, I want God on my side! I want to have a humble attitude. It is too easy to be impressed by our own accomplishments and forget Who is the real Source of all the good in our lives.

I want to die to my pride, and receive my self-worth from my relationship with God. He is the Source of all the good things in my life. Knowing Who God is and that He has given us all we have, keeps us on the right road to having a correct and humble attitude in our Worship.

Joy

When my grandkids look up at me and smile, it lights up my heart. Jesus said,

"I have come that their joy might be full!"
John 15:11, 16:24

God loves it when His children are full of joy. Too many times in life, we feel beaten down. Too many times we feel defeated. God doesn't want us to feel that way! He wants us to remember that He is on our side. He wants us to remind ourselves of how far we have come. He wants to remind us of how many victories He has already accomplished in our lives.

God wants us to come into our Worship times with joyful songs. Psalm 100 says it this way:

Worship the LORD with gladness. Come before Him, singing with joy. Acknowledge that the LORD is God. He made us, and we are His.
Psalm 100:2-3

With Our Whole Hearts

I often put this slogan on my weekly Worship lists:

Do things with passion, or not at all.
Wherever you go, go with all your heart.

God commands us to love Him with all our heart, soul, mind, and strength. Frankly I don't want to go through life without passion. I want to be someone who puts my whole heart and being into what I am doing. Whether I am playing tennis, riding my mountain-bike, writing music, studying, or spending time with my family – I want to do it with my whole heart!

God wants our worship and our love for Him to be with our whole heart. As a musician, I think it's a crime to do music without passion. As a lover of God, I think it's a crime to only be "going through the motions" in our Worship. God deserves so much more!

Human beings have a huge range of attitudes. We want to make sure that when we come into God's presence, we come with great attitudes. We want to be thankful, honest, reverent, joyful, humble, and with hearts full of faith. God deserves our whole hearts!

24: KEYS TO LONGEVITY IN MINISTRY

I recently celebrated 40 years since I started into full-time ministry. Along the way, there have been some incredible highs and a few lows, but I have always been amazed at the faithfulness of God. Here are a few things I have learned about running the race.

Spend Time With God Daily

God is the Source of all good things, so it certainly makes sense to spend time with Him daily. One of the best habits I have developed is opening my Bible early every morning and spending time getting to know God through His Word. It helps me keep my eyes on the Lord, through good times and bad times. God's Word has taught me about wisdom, faith, love, relationships, integrity, forgiveness, leadership, and a host of other invaluable life lessons. I could not have survived without spending time with God daily.

Family and Friends

The Lord has blessed me with great family and friends. I have great parents, grandparents and in-laws. I have a Godly wife who has been an awesome support throughout our journey. When we have peaceful, loving, healthy homes, we have great places to retreat to when the fireworks go off! Family is so important. Good friends are important. Invest in our spouses, our children, extended family, and friends. It pays great dividends. We may change churches, but we always keep the same families.

Work on Improving Daily

None of us starts with all the gifts and talents we need. Great mentors, education, seminars, books, positive feedback, and daily discipline are all part of what it takes to stay on a journey of improvement. Never stop growing. If we don't keep growing, chances are we won't last long. In the Parable of the Talents (see Matthew 25), the person who didn't double his talents got the boot!

Forgive

Hurts will come. Conflict will happen. It is inevitable. To survive the race, we need to learn to forgive quickly and often. Learn to deal with conflict the Jesus way! Learn to overcome our reticence to go to people directly. A lot of problems can be solved with one-on-one conversations. Even when we don't feel like it, forgive. God has forgiven us! It is the only healthy way to move forward. We will not survive in ministry if we don't forgive.

Humility

Keeping the right attitude in life is huge! We want to have the confidence that comes with walking with the Creator of the Universe, but we need the humility that comes with knowing that any of us can fail. Put in the safeguards in our lives that will help us to keep a proper perspective and attitude. Be humble. Be accountable.

Build Great Teams

If we are doing it right, we'll find the job is way too big to do by ourselves. One of my great joys in ministry has been to develop great teams of people to work with: production teams ... music teams ... choirs ... bands ... Alpha teams ... sound teams ... technical teams ... and on and on! Out of those teams will grow leaders – leaders whom God will use, and will often send out. Jesus said, "*Go into all the world*" (Mark 16:15). Our job is to train people to go!

Recharge

When God created the Universe, He took a day off. If God needs a day off, so do we! I have always made a point of taking days off, and also having great vacation times with the family. Life flies by. I love the memories we have created in our vacation times together.

Also, we look after our health. I have learned the value of regular exercise and proper diet. Life is a marathon, not a sprint.

You will keep in perfect peace all who trust in You, all whose thoughts are fixed on You!
Isaiah 23:6

25: I LOVE LISTS. AND SO DOES GOD.

I am a list guy. I love to make lists.

- Lists of what I want to do
- Lists of music that I have done
- Lists of music I still want to do
- Lists of family
- Lists of musicians I work with
- Lists of people in my life, including their emails, addresses and phone numbers
- Lists of places I have been
- Lists of places I would still like to see
- Lists of my goals
- Lists of what I want to do before I kick the bucket (the "Bucket List")
- Lists of my prayers.

So many lists! I am a list guy.

Do you like to make lists? I find them kind of handy. Lists help organize my thoughts. Lists help me to keep my life manageable. Lists help me stay on track; they help me make sense of all the activities going on around me.

It seems that God likes lists also. Quite often throughout the Bible, you'll see lists of people, lists of families and genealogies, lists of materials to build buildings, and lists of commandments.

The most famous list is in Exodus 20:1-17 –
the Ten Commandments:

1. *Put God first*
2. *Worship God only*
3. *Use God's Name with respect*
4. *Remember to take a day off every week*
5. *Respect and honor your parents*
6. *Do not hurt other people*
7. *Be faithful in marriage*
8. *Do not steal*
9. *Do not lie*
10. *Do not be envious of others.*

What a great list! Jesus even made that list
simpler. I just love it when we can simplify life!
Jesus said that living a great life really boils down
to two main things:

A. *Love God with all your heart, soul, mind, and strength*
B. *Love your neighbor as yourself.*

I like that list! I have decided to live by those
lists. They make sense to me. I am a list guy.

26: DOES GOD SING?

I love Music. I have discovered that God also loves Music. The largest book of the Bible is the Book of Psalms – which are lyrics from 150 songs.

I love singing. God also loves singing. In the Old Testament, we read about God singing over us:

> *For the LORD your God is living among you. He is a mighty Savior. He will take delight in you with gladness. With His love, He will calm all your fears. He will rejoice over you with joyful songs.*
>
> **Zephaniah 3:17**

I love musical instruments, At my house, you will discover about a dozen musical instruments that I love to play. I discovered that God also loves musical instruments. In the Psalms, it frequently talks about using all kinds of instruments to give praise to God:

> *Praise God with the lyre and harp! Praise Him with the tambourine and dancing; praise Him with strings and flutes! Praise Him with a clash of cymbals; praise Him with loud clanging cymbals. Let everything that breathes sing praises*

to the LORD! Praise the LORD!

Psalm 150:3-6

I love to sing praises to God. It is good to note that some of God's most beloved men also loved to sing praises to God. Men like Moses, David and Solomon were all song-writers and singers who loved to sing praises to God:

Let all that I am praise the LORD. I will praise the LORD as long as I live. I will sing praises to my God with my dying breath.

Psalm 146:1-2

Never be shy about singing your praises to God. Our Redeemer loves it when we sing to Him. Singing has a way of expressing our deepest feelings and emotions. Lifting your voice to God in song is a powerful way to give Him the worship He so richly deserves!

27: THE SECRET TO LEARNING DIFFICULT SKILLS

Have you ever seen a musician or an athlete and wonder how they got that good? Each of us are born with different talents, but none becomes experts at something overnight. That is where diligence and personal discipline separates people who are good and people who are great.

It wasn't until I was in university that I really learned the secret to conquering difficult skills. It is a secret that can be transferred into many areas of study. Here is the secret:

**Break down the difficult skill
into daily bite-sized pieces.**

What part of that difficult skill or task can you learn today? Then daily, step by step, slowly add to your skill level until you conquer it.

Here's an example from my musical studies. I once had to learn an extremely difficult piece of piano music that was around 80 bars long. It was way above my skill level. But I realized that I could learn the first two or three bars today if I slowly broke them down and spent a couple of hours practicing. I would learn the right hand for the first few bars, then I would learn the left hand for the same section. Then I would slowly put the hands together at quarter-speed and slowly increase the speed until I had learned those few bars perfectly.

Over a matter of a few months of working on the music daily, I gradually learned more and more bars, until I had mastered that entire piece of music. It was a matter of learning a bit more each day, in a disciplined manner. I simply learned how to practice properly and diligently. I learned not to practice my mistakes, but to slowly learn something bit by bit, daily adding to that knowledge.

It's a powerful principle. I have applied it to learning new sports ... to memorizing large portions of the Bible ... and to orchestrating large musical scores with dozens of musical instruments. It works for so many areas of life.

Learn to break down the larger problem or challenge into bite-sized chunks. Learn to tackle that project daily, and build on the success of the day before. It is amazing what difficult skills and projects we can conquer if we gradually develop the skills and knowledge on a daily basis.

God has given us amazing minds and bodies. If we apply great discipline, diligence and wisdom, it is astonishing what we can do. It is satisfying what difficult skills we can master.

Discipline is the bridge between goals and accomplishments.

~ **Jim Rohn**

All athletes are disciplined in their training. They do it to win a prize that will fade away but we do it for an eternal prize.

~ **The Apostle Paul,** 1 Corinthians 9:25-27

The discipline you learn and the character you build from setting and achieving a goal can be more valuable than the achievement of the goal itself.

~ **Bo Bennett,** *Tech Guru*

We all naturally want to become successful ... we also want to take shortcuts. And it's easy to do so, but you can never take away the effort of hard work, discipline and sacrifice.

~ **Apolo Ohno,**
Olympic Gold Medal Speed Skater

We must all suffer one of two things: the pain of discipline, or the pain of regret or disappointment. The difference is discipline weighs ounces, while regret weighs tons!

~ **Jim Rohn**

28: PICKING NEW SONGS FOR WORSHIP

Picking great songs for worship is one of the most important skills a worship leader needs to learn. There are many different kinds and levels of songs. Some songs are written **about** God, some are written to express our feelings, some are sung prayers, some are upbeat praise songs, and some are pure worship **to** God.

There are fast songs, medium-tempo songs and slow songs. There are difficult songs and easy songs. But what are the best songs for us to sing with our congregations? What songs help our congregations to sing with all their hearts and connect with God?

Distilled from my years of a variety of experiences musically, here is my philosophy of picking Worship songs:

(1) **Learn to pick great songs, not just doable ones.** Great songs are those we will still be singing a year from now. Different songs have a different "shelf life." Some we don't mind singing a few times, but after that, we seem to forget them. Generally speaking, a congregation learns about 20 to 25 songs per year, so make them great songs.

(2) One of the tests of a "great song" is that **you catch yourself singing it by yourself,** in your car, in your house, when you are out on a walk. Or a congregational member tells you that all week, they have been singing that new song we introduced last weekend. Or we hear our spouses singing that new song.

(3) **Great songs have the Spirit of God resting on them.** This is a little harder to quantify. When I hear a great song, I sense God. The song moves my heart. I realize that God is in the song. Combine that with praying and asking God what songs to sing will lead us in the right direction.

(4) I love to pick great songs **from around the world.** God is moving on anointed musicians and writers from around the globe. We now have access online to worship bands in Australia, Canada, the United States, England, Europe, Asia, and Africa. I don't want to limit my song choices to one church or one church-movement.

(5) It is easier than ever to **learn what churches around the world are singing.** *CCLI* has an invaluable online list of the top 200 songs which churches are singing. Their *Top SongSelect List* shows what thousands of other

worship leaders are picking for their congregations. If you are wondering what songs to sing, let me assure you that the songs on this list are like gold.

(6) There are certain writers who have been **writing great songs for years** – Matt Redman ... Chris Tomlin ... Paul Baloche ... Reuben Morgan ... Joel Houston ... Tim Hughes ... and Brenton Brown have consistently written great songs; and there are some great newcomers: **Ben Cantelon ... Brian Johnson ... Matt Maher ... Jesse Reeves ... Phil Wickham,** and many others.

(7) Learn to keep a **balanced repertoire.** We need fast songs, medium-paced songs and slow songs. Make sure to continue to pick great songs of different tempos that fill the need. **Keep it fresh.**

(8) Learn to **repeat new songs enough times** for the congregation to learn them. My philosophy is to:

(a) teach the new song the first week;
(b) always repeat the new song the next week;
(c) give it a week off;

(d) then repeat it again the fourth week. That way, the congregation is hearing the new song three times over a four-week period.

If it is a great song, the congregation will know it by then. It also helps if the song is on Christian radio because the congregation is also hearing it their cars and their homes.

(9) Put the **songs in keys the congregation can sing.** Most people do not have a huge vocal range. If in doubt, use the "rule of D" principle, making the top note around a D (C-Eb).

(10) By all means, **use original songs** that are birthed in our congregations. But my advice is to be certain the songs match the quality of the rest of your list. I generally use only one original song per set, with the rest of the list being great songs from around the world.

(11) Make sure **the melody is singable and memorable.** *"Does the song work without the band?"* ... *"Does the song work with just a simple acoustic guitar or piano?"* ... *"Do we find ourselves singing the song when we're by ourselves?"*

(12) **Start and end strong!** I usually start a Worship set with an upbeat Praise song which

people can easily connect with, and I usually end with a slower great Worship song which is sung directly to God. I never start or end with a brand-new song, no matter how good it is. In between, I am working on transitioning musically and thematically, with my main purpose of having the congregation focusing on and meeting God in our short time together each week.

Shout with joy to the LORD, all the Earth! Worship the LORD with gladness. Come before Him, singing with joy. Acknowledge that the LORD is God! He made us, and we are His. We are His people, the sheep of His pasture. Enter His gates with thanksgiving; go into His courts with praise. Give thanks to Him and praise His Name. For the LORD is good. His unfailing love continues forever, and His faithfulness continues to each generation.

Psalm 100:1-5

29: RUNNING A WORSHIP BAND REHEARSAL

I have spent many days and evenings at rehearsals. It is the price you pay if you want to do Music at a good musical level. It is the price you pay if you want to get past the music and be able to worship God freely. I have had rehearsals with orchestras ... choirs ... marching bands ... brass and string sections ... and Worship bands in Europe ... Asia ... Australia ... Africa ... the Caribbean ... and North America. Along the way, I have picked up a few ideas on how to have a good rehearsal. Here is what I have learned so far:

Rehearsal Space

Preparation for a rehearsal starts long before the actual rehearsal. First, you need to get a good rehearsal space. Depending on the size of the group, this could be your house, a recording or rehearsal studio, a church, or a hall auditorium. Things to consider include good lighting, ventilation, acoustics, and musical and sound equipment.

Musicians

Next, you need to organize the people you need to come to the rehearsal. That usually happens weeks ahead, through e-mails, texts and phone calls. People are busy. Make sure you give all involved the necessary lead-time for them to be there. With my church Worship team and sound people, I usually book them 4- to 8-weeks in advance.

Songs

Picking the songs is another important step in the process. Questions that you should ask yourself include:

- *"Are these the best Worship songs for this situation?"*
- *"Will these songs work for my congregation?"*
- *"What does God want?"*
- *"Can the band and the singers successfully perform this style?"*
- *"Is this the best key for this song?"*
- *"What is the best tempo and metronome marking for this song?"*

Charts

Next, you need to prepare the charts. Different bands operate with different charts. In my early years, we didn't have charts – we played everything by ear. Someone led the song, and we just picked it up by listening; later, someone wrote out the music, and we followed while reading the chart. Today, many Worship bands use lyrics topped with the chords. Personally, I prefer a full vocal chart with notes, lyrics, form, and chords. The more time you spend working on a great chart and arrangement, the less time you need to work on explaining those details to the band in your rehearsal. Great charts make for a much more efficient rehearsal.

Also, I never use other people's charts. Most charts have mistakes! I always make my own charts, and tailor them to how I want the music to go. I also make special *capo* parts for acoustic guitar players.

Distributing Charts

Once the charts are written, I put them online in *Dropbox* in a .pdf form, and either give the band the links to download or I directly e-mail them. Then I send little messages to the players about which areas will probably need their attention. Also, I photocopy all the charts and bring them with me to the rehearsal.

Pre-Rehearsal

The sooner the band gets the charts and links to the music (such as via MP3s or *YouTube*), the more chance they have to rehearse. My habit has been to send out the music for Sunday on the Monday before (example: for Sunday July 13th, charts are sent on Monday July 6th). My midweek rehearsals have usually been on Thursdays, which gives the musicians and singers four days to prepare. Some people send out lists weeks in advance, but personally I find that most people don't actually rehearse until a day or two before the rehearsal.

Leader's Preparation

The next most important step is the personal preparation of the leader. As a leader, you should know the music inside and out. I take time to know what the drummer's groove should be ... the basic bass patterns ... what each vocalist should be singing ... and the form of the song, including the intro, ending and exact tempo. Other areas to know would be the lead lines for the keyboards and the lead guitar, and the basic strumming and playing patterns you want each player to play. The more you know the music and what you want from each player and singer, the better results you will get.

The Rehearsal

The next step is the actual rehearsal. Start and end on time! Be highly organized and keep the rehearsal moving. Make sure everyone tunes their instruments ahead of time. Start with the new material while the energy level is higher. Know the potential problem areas of the music before you get there. Expect and foster a Christian attitude among the band members. Treat others the way you want to be treated. Communicate clearly. Pray. Spend time worshipping God. Remember: your actual goal is to worship God, not just do music well.

Listening

As a leader, it is important to really listen. Don't get so caught up in your own playing and singing that you don't listen to the whole arrangement.

- *"Is something out of tune?"*
- *"Is someone playing the wrong chord or note?"*
- *"Is that the right tempo?"*
- *"Is someone dragging or rushing?"*
- *"Is the groove for that song correct?"*
- *"How is the vocal and band balance?"*
- *"Is someone too loud?"*
- *"Is the band too busy?"*

Great music has ebbs and flows; learn the dynamics of the song. *"When should the different players be sitting out of a section of the music?"* Generally speaking, the band will only get to the level that you expect from them.

Excellence

Don't be afraid to challenge the singers and players to play to the best of their ability. People want to be part of something good. Learn to speak the truth in love. Challenge people to practice the music and memorize it. Expect excellence!

Here are some final tests for your worship, music and rehearsal:

- *"Is this song really working at a musical level?"*
- *"Does this music minister to people and work for your congregation?"*
- *"Are the band and singers just playing music, or are they also worshipping God?"*
- *"Does this music glorify God, and do you sense God is in this music?"*

30: I LOVE WRITING SONGS TO GOD

When my son Josh was going to a Christian school, one of his assignments was to memorize Bible passages. One evening, I helped him memorize Psalm 139. What a powerful psalm! After a few hours of working with Josh, he went to bed ... and then God started ministering **to me** through those ancient lyrics.

You have searched me, LORD, and You know me
You know when I sit and when I rise
You perceive my thoughts from afar
Where can I go from Your Spirit?
Where can I flee from Your presence?
If I go up to the heavens, You are there
If I make my bed in the depths, You are there
If I rise on the wings of the dawn
If I settle on the far side of the sea
Even there Your hand will guide me
Your right hand will hold me fast.

As I read those incredible lyrics, a melody came to me. For the next few hours, I wrote my own version of Psalm 139 to the Lord. I remember the tears rolling down my face as the power of David's words touched my heart. It is astounding that God – Who created the Heavens and the Earth – knows me! He loves me! His Spirit is always with me – how amazing!

My heart's desire is to live a life that is pleasing to Him. The Psalmist David said it this way:

Search me, God, and know my heart
Test me and know my anxious thoughts
See if there is any offensive way in e
And lead me in the way everlasting.

I love writing songs to God!

Psalm 139

Oh Lord, You have searched my heart
And You know my thoughts, my ways
When I sit and when I rise
Oh Lord, before I speak
You know my words
Your ways are too marvelous for me

Where can I go, oh Lord
From Your Spirit?
Where can I hide
From Your presence?
If I rise on the wings of the morning dawn
If I settle on the edge of the sea

If I go to the depths of the deepest sea
If I rise to the heavens above
Even there Your hands will hold me close

Even there Your hands will guide me.

King David said it first, and I entirely agree –
and we both praise our wonderful Heavenly
Father. I would love to hear his version of this
song one day ... maybe even get to sing along with
him!

31: TAKING SUNDAY MORNING WORSHP TO THE NEXT LEVEL

I love leading God's people in Worship. I have been blessed to have led church Worship teams at home (in Canada) and around the world for over 25 years. Here are a few things I have learned along that way.

Pick Great Songs

Picking great songs of Worship is so important. They should be singable, memorable, Biblical, and inspirational. Great songs of Worship have a God-dynamic all their own.

Congregations often rush to church, trying to get there on time, and are frequently unfocused on God. One of my jobs is to pick great songs that help them focus on Him as soon as possible. That usually works best by finding an uptempo Worship tune that is easy to sing and gets them engaged as soon as possible.

I usually have 30 minutes to do Worship in a Sunday morning service, so for my team that mean five songs. My general plan is to do two uptempo songs – often more Praise-oriented, and usually the second song is slightly faster than the first. Then I do a strong medium-tempo transition song. Then I end with two powerful Worship songs that are sung directly to God.

This general guideline helps the congregation to go from focusing and singing **about** God ... to worshipping God **directly**. It is not meant to be a "formula" but an overriding time-proven way to help achieve the goal of getting the congregation to focus their hearts and worship on God.

Have Great Rehearsals

I normally have two-and-a-half hours of rehearsal for every 30 minutes of Worship time. The goal is to become so proficient at doing the music that we do not have to think about the music during the live Worship time. We need to get past simply "performing" music, to focusing on and worshiping God!

Normal practice is to have a strong, two-hour mid-week rehearsal (Thursday night is my favorite) and then a 45-minute rehearsal on Sunday morning. These rehearsal times gives everyone time to learn the music properly and work out any problem areas.

Work on Great Sound and Media

A good sound-man can make or break you! There is no use having great songs and rehearsals if the sound-mix is not working for the congregation. Putting the drums in a full "cage" generally helps get the best overall mix. Also, putting baffles around guitar amps and the band wearing in-ear monitors really helps the sound-man. I also try to take a Sunday off the stage once a month, to listen to the front-of-house mix.

In the same way, having a media-person who is on top of the projected lyrics is huge. Besides having the lyrics-screen up front for the congregation, we also have a large screen at the back of the auditorium for the singers to see the lyrics too.

If we have the sound-man giving us a great mix and the media operator giving the lyrics at the right time, we have a strong sound and visual foundation on which to work!

Put God First

Worshipping God is a daily lifestyle. If we are just worshipping God on Sunday mornings, we are living a sub-par Christian lifestyle. Sunday mornings should just be the tip of the iceberg!

When we honor God daily by reading His Word, praying, worshipping, spending time with Him – He will honor us by showing up Sunday mornings in our corporate Worship times.

We are capable of putting together a good band and a great song list ... but only God can touch people's hearts and heal their bodies and minds. Put God first in our daily lives, and He will show up in powerful ways in our Sunday morning corporate Worship.

Also, put God first in your actual Worship time. Sometimes we can get so caught up in the music, the transitions, the mechanics of leading and playing that we don't focus on the main thing: God! God is why we come together, God is why we sing great songs and worship. God is the reason. Don't allow the distractions of live music get in the way of worshipping God with all our hearts and leading our congregations to do the same!

Memorize Your Music

There are few things worse than seeing a Worship leader and his team whose eyes are glued to their music. When we memorize the music, we can communicate better with the congregation and with God! To get past the music, we need to memorize it, and know it so well that we do not have to think about it. Great teams and leaders memorize the music so they can worship freely.

Worship God With All Your Heart

The first and greatest commandment is to love the Lord your God with all our heart, mind, soul, and strength. This includes worshipping God with our actions. The actions of Biblical Worship include singing, clapping, raising our hands, dancing, bowing, and shouting. We serve an awesome God Who created every good thing that we enjoy. He is worthy of passionate worship.

Never let ourselves just go through the motions of singing a song. Be a passionate worshipper who loves and worships God with all you have. Learn to incorporate all the actions of Worship into our personal and corporate Worship!

Be a Great Example to Our Congregations

Congregations tend to mirror the passion of the Worship team. If the people up front are full of passion and energy for worshipping God, the congregation tends to lift their Worship to a higher level.

We have the opportunity to be passionate examples of worshippers to our congregations. If they see us and the team worshipping God with our whole hearts, souls, minds, and strength on a weekly basis, they will grow in their passion for Worship.

If we lead, they will follow. It sometimes does not happen immediately, but that is what Worship leadership is about. A big part of leadership is helping people grow in their passion and worship of God. Learn to be a passionate worshipper of God, on and off the stage. Be authentic, and do not lose your passion for loving and worshipping God with all our hearts!

32: HOW TO LEARN A MUSICAL INSTRUMENT

Over the years, I have heard numerous people comment on how they wish they could play a musical instrument. Along my way, I have learned to play over a dozen instruments. My love of playing instruments and worshipping God has opened the door for me to travel around the world numerous times. Here are a few tips to help us be successful.

Get Started

It is no good to just wish we could do something. We can do anything if we have the right plan, and motivation, and put consistent effort into it. So just start! Here's how:

The way to get started is to quit talking and begin doing.

~ **Walt Disney**

Buy or Rent a Decent Instrument

What instrument are you thinking about learning? There are dozens. What instrument inspires you: piano, guitar, saxophone, violin, drums? If you are not sure which instrument to buy, ask an experienced musician.

The instruments I own vary from a $25 harmonica, to a $90 ukulele, to a $700 guitar, to a $2,500 saxophone (three of those), to a $7,000 grand piano. Generally speaking, the more money we invest in an instrument, the easier it is to play and the better it sounds.

Another way to initially go is to rent an instrument. Most music stores will gladly rent a decent instrument until you find out whether you like it and will stick with it, or not.

Get a Good Teacher

Good teachers are worth their weight in gold. They will help you proceed quickly and efficiently ... will keep you accountable and motivated ... and will help you over various stumbling blocks, and be able to answer your questions.

These days, you can also learn from *YouTube* and various video series. They are extremely helpful and cheaper. But to be successful, you must be very disciplined. Most people aren't that disciplined, so a (live) teacher is still the best way to go!

Find At Least One Hour Per Day to Practice

You can have the best teacher in the world, but if you do not discipline yourself to practice, you will not progress very far or very quickly. Life is busy, but somehow people always find time to watch TV and do the stuff they like. Carve out an hour a day from your schedule ... and make that hour sacred. Daily, consistent practice is the only way to be successful in learning music.

Get Passionate About It!

You will only stick with something you are passionate and even obsessive about it. When I was first learning piano, it was not unusual for me to spend two to four hours a day practicing. With every instrument I learned, I would put in consistent practice time until I got to the level where I was happy.

Right now, I am learning a non-musical skill: I am trying to learn to be a good tennis player. And I am using the same principles of playing and practicing daily, often up to 10 to 15 hours per week. In the last year, I have seen my skill level increase 75%, and I even won our club championship for my level.

Do Not Give Up!

Skill comes from consistently adding to what you learned the day before. The secret to getting good at anything is **to not give up!** I started learning musical instruments when I was a child, and I just never quit. Along the way, I have seen people who were equally as talented ... but they gave up. They quit. I just never did.

If you believe in yourself and have dedication and pride – and never quit – you'll be a winner. The price of victory is high, but so are the rewards.

~ **Paul Bryant**

33: WORKING WITH A BILLIONAIRE

When I was a teenager, I played saxophone and clarinet in an old-fashioned church orchestra at my home church, *Glad Tidings,* in Vancouver. Jimmy Pattison, a local business man who was a millionaire (and who later became a billionaire and one of Canada's richest people) attended our church, and was asked to direct our very unpolished group for a season.

His leadership changed everything! Mr. Pattison was – and is – a fantastic motivator. First, he didn't tolerate people being late. If you were one minute late, then don't bother coming. Suddenly, everyone was early for rehearsal.

Secondly, Mr. Pattison knew how to bring fun and passion to a rehearsal. We didn't have proper orchestration or written-out parts like I provide for people now. We just winged it. He would photocopy some upbeat hymn, and we learned to transpose our parts "on the fly." Then he would suddenly point at someone during the rehearsal, and he would be expected to stand up and play a solo.

If his solo bombed, he sat back down. But if his solo had potential, then Mr. Pattison would let you play it in the live church service that night, in front of 800 to 1,000 people. Soon I was always thinking ahead of what I would play if and when he pointed at me. I bombed a few times, but for the most part, I got better and better at improvising a solo on the spot. It was fun!

That "play well or bomb under pressure" ideology became a great challenge. There were several of us who became regular soloists. He would point to a strong violinist, or ask for a drum solo, or point to an accordion, piano, sax, or trumpet player. It was always fun to see who would rise to the occasion and who would bomb. You would get some friendly ribbing if you bombed. It was all part of the fun and excitement of playing with Mr. Pattison.

Mr. Pattison also taught me about generosity; his giving is legendary. One Sunday morning, when we were raising money to build a new church, he came to the front and gave his personal testimony on giving ... and then he donated $500,000. His donation was matched by another family in the church, and together they challenged the whole church to match their donations. Total pledges that morning were over $2,700,000.

When *Glad Tidings* had its 75th Anniversary, I was asked to come back home and lead Worship. In the service, I introduced Mr. Pattison to play a trumpet solo (*"Was it sweet revenge?"*). Earlier in that service, there had been an offering taken to put a new roof on the church; I believe the goal was $125,000. When Mr. Pattison came up to play, he first told the chairman that he would top off whatever didn't come in that offering. Off the top of his head, he probably donated $50,000 to $70,000. Wow!

His testimony told of meeting with his chief financial officer when his business was in a slump. He wanted to know how much they had been *giving* because he realized that his success came from the Lord, and he didn't want to get behind in his giving.

My children and family benefitted immensely from Mr. Pattison's generosity and vision. He built and funded *Pacific Academy*, one of the premier private Christian schools in Canada. I have no idea of how many millions of dollars he poured into that institution, but my kids reaped the benefits of a world-class Christian education in a world-class facility.

"Thank you, Mr. Pattison, you are an inspiration!"

34: GUIDELINES FOR A STRONG WORSHIP TEAM

In any quality organization, there are codes of conduct and concrete expectations. A number of years ago, I attended a Worship Conference at *Gateway Church* in Dallas, and I was totally impressed by their Worship team. Based on *Gateway's* code of conduct and my own experience, here are my standards and guidelines for my Worship teams.

Guidelines for Worship Ministry

- Must have a personal relationship with Jesus Christ that is consistent and growing through prayer, Bible reading and church fellowship.

- Be a committed attendee and tither of our church, including regular attendance at Sunday services.

- Demonstrate technical competence as either a singer, musician or audio/media technician.

- Singers and musicians must be comfortable on stage, and expressive in their praise and worship before God.

- Maintain a faithful attendance record.

- Be committed to practicing an hour or more per week at home on their Sunday songs.

Commitment to a Godly Lifestyle

- Worship team members are expected to live a lifestyle that is above reproach, avoiding even *"the appearance of evil"* (1 Timothy 3:3). Being a minister who is up front adds extra responsibilities because people see us as examples of what a Christian should be like. Therefore it is imperative we consider the way we treat each other and carefully guard our hearts from impurities and pride.

- It is God's desire and our desire to see our Worship team members living a victorious Christian life, free from bondage. If there are any addictions or issues with which you struggle, please let us know – we are here to help you, not to judge you.

- The following issues should be dealt with before any public ministry position is taken:

  - alcohol and drug abuse;
  - sexual immorality;
  - prideful attitude; anger and rage problems;
  - inability to submit to leadership; gossiping and stirring up strife;

- an unbiblical lifestyle.

Dress Code

General dress code: modest and dressy, culturally relevant styles are key.

- No overly tight clothing. No short skirts or dresses.
- No sleeveless tops (without a covering).
- No revealing clothing (such as see-through material without an undershirt or camisole).
- Proper footwear: polished shoes or dressy running shoes.
- No gaudy or oversized jewelry (anything that might be a distraction).

Sunday Morning Attire

- **Men:** Collared shirt and slacks; optional jackets, sweaters and/or vests.

- **Ladies:** Blouse and slacks, skirt or dress (knee-length). No pants that are tight all the way to the ankle unless you wear a long top that goes mid-thigh. No gaucho or cropped pants of any kind.

- **All:** Nice dark dress jeans are also acceptable. Old and baggy jeans are not acceptable. If in doubt, wear dress pants. No hats.

- **Colors:** Stick to neutral tones (black, all gray tones, browns and similar tones, light or dark blue, dark purple, white and off-white). No loud prints.

Schedule Requirements

- Typically each band member and singer will be scheduled twice per month, based on their availability and monthly service schedules.

- Arriving on time and ready for practice is essential for each member! In order to present Worship music that is both excellent in quality and anointed, a strong rehearsal is necessary. The more we practice, the freer we are to worship and lead others into Worship.

- **Mandatory** Thursday Night Rehearsals: 7:30 to 9:30pm * **(Note:** Only that Sunday's team practices on the Thursday night prior.)

Tips For Better Platform Presence

- Look in the mirror and watch what you look like – jump, clap, bow, dance, raise your hands, be engaging. If something appears awkward, adjust it to make sure you are communicating what you intend to communicate.

- Do not let the congregation determine your level of expression; sometimes they will not be engaged in worship. As leaders, we always need to be engaged. Show them an example of how to express worship. Most of the time, they simply need to see genuine worship in order to learn how to express it on their own.

- Be sincere. Worship from your heart. Give a warm smile from within. We are leading people from all different circumstances, so remember that a warm smile ministers more than you realize.

- Musicians – Be sure you stay engaged in Worship. Practice ahead of time so you don't have to focus on your instrument the whole time. Sing while you play. Seeing a musician singing from their heart can really help people worship. Move around your area. Use your space to the fullest; when there is no movement, the platform can look stagnant.

35: IMPROVING YOUR SINGING

For many decades, I have worked with singers of average talent to singers with great talent, on the road, in the recording studio, in church, and in other musical settings. Here is what I have learned so far about helping singers improve:

Learn to Breathe Properly

Learning to breathe deeply and with control is the foundation of singing. I played saxophone for many years, which really helped develop my lungs and diaphragm. The diaphragm is the muscle that controls pushing air from our lungs.

Warm-up Your Voice Before Singing

As a Worship leader, one of my chief times to sing is on Sunday morning. Unfortunately, it takes time to warm up my voice, and mornings are not always the best time. One of my favorite tricks, while driving to rehearsal, is to sing along in a soft voice with the songs on my MP3 player, sometimes down an octave. It took me around 20 minutes to drive to church, so it was a great warm-up.

Sing Every Day

Like most things in life, we improve by doing it daily. Do not be shy about singing in your car or singing around your house. When I was on the road and we were singing and performing 6 or 7 times per week, it was amazing how strong our voices got. *"Use it, or lose it."*

Copy Your Favorite Singers

There are many different kinds of singers and styles of music. Most singers start off by copying their favorite artists, and then developing their own style from there. That is normal. Get out your favorite recordings and copy their tone, inflections and vibrato. Copying great singers is one of the best ways to learn and grow.

Take Singing Lessons

Sometimes you can only go so far on our own. A good teacher will help with breathing, tone, intonation, posture, and a host of other important details. We still have to practice every day, but they will help correct the things we may be doing wrongly.

Learn How to Project Your Voice
When You Sing

We can't sing loudly if we do not breathe properly. Once we had an internationally-known opera singer visit our house. I asked her to sing, and it felt like our house shifted on its foundation from her awesome tone and volume. Good tone comes from learning how to project your voice. Go for it! Don't be shy, sing loudly!

Learn to Sing With Passion

Great singers know how to sing with emotion. If we love a song and sing it from our hearts, it should show in the emotions we present. It should show in our stage presence. As a singer who loves to worship God, there are few things as powerful as singing with passion to the Creator of the universe.

Learn to Listen For Pitch Problems

Few things are worse than someone singing out of tune. Learn to sing along with your favorite recordings, or with your piano, and really try to match the pitch. Practically everyone can learn to sing in tune with constant practice and listening.

Drink Lots of Water

Keeping your voice healthy and lubricated is important! Room temperature water is the best way to keep our voices well-lubricated. Avoid caffeine, dairy products and alcohol before we sing. Those liquids generally hurt more than they help.

Record Yourself Singing

Generally speaking, no one likes the recorded sound of their own voice. But listening to recordings of yourself really is the best way to truly hear what you sound like. It is the best way to pick up on how well your pitch, vibrato and breath control works. Don't be discouraged because you sound different than your voice sounds in your head. This is a common problem for everyone. Keep listening, keep growing, keep improving.

36: IMPROVING WORSHIP LEADING

Through trial-and-experience, continually exercising my musical skills, growing deeper in my relationship with God – Who is so worthy of our praise! – here are steps to improving your Worship leading.

Study Under a Great Worship Leader

This is the best way to learn, and it can take on many forms. Jesus used this method to teach His disciples. They ministered alongside Him for three years, and then He sent them out to do it themselves.

If we have good mentors in our church, watch and learn from them. In this situation, we can watch them in weekly rehearsals and Sunday morning Worship times. Study what makes them successful, and learn from their strengths and weaknesses.

If we're not blessed with good mentors in our local churches, seek out a mentor. This can take many forms. We can go to Worship conferences, watch those leaders, attend their classes or workshops. We can go to local Worship events and watch those leaders. As opportunities arise, we can attend other churches, and note what each church does well ... and what they do not so well. We can also check out *YouTube* videos of Worship leaders, and note their different styles and ways of leading Worship.

Make Worshipping God a Daily Part of Our Life

Anything we can do daily, we will improve upon. Spending time with God on a daily basis is an essential prerequisite for being a Worship leader. This should include daily time reading our Bibles. My habit has been to read a Psalm and a Proverb every day, and I use a daily reading plan that takes me through the whole Bible each year.

Reading the whole Bible every year will give you an overview of how God works in people's lives. I have read the Bible through every year for the last 30-plus years, and God's Word still speaks to me *"new every morning"* (Lamentations 3:23). The Bible has a way of being relevant for the situation you are going through right now.

Another important part of spending time with God is in prayer. A well-known pastor once said, *"The key to my prayer life is that I pray and I obey."* The key to prayer is finding what God wants us to do, and then doing it.

As we spend time with God daily, we will know Him better and love Him more. And our passion for worship will increase. The best Worship leaders worship God much more privately than they do publicly. Our public ministry should only be the tip of the iceberg.

Learn the Great Worship Songs

There are great Worship songs coming from all over the Earth. There has never been a better time to learn Worship songs. We now have access to great songs and recordings from around the world. We now have websites full of the great songs that God is using.

Learn the old songs and the new songs. **Memorize** these songs. Find the songs God's Spirit is resting on. Find the songs that are blessing the nations.

A great place to find the strongest Worship songs is to look at the lists which *CCLI* has compiled. With the honest participation and reporting of local churches globally, they track the songs which are sung in many countries around the world. Check out their "*SongSelect Top 200*" list; it's a great list of current songs.

Understand the Progression of Worship

I will enter His gates with thanksgiving, and into His courts with praise.

Psalm 100:4

God likes it when we come before Him with singing. One of the most common ways to begin a Worship service is with songs of thanksgiving.

These songs are often sung **about** God (generally known as "Praise" songs), as opposed to songs which sing directly **to** God (generally known as "Worship" songs). (Technically, a Worship leader is actually a *"Praise and Worship"* leader.) Praise songs are often – but not exclusively – faster in tempo and praise-oriented. If often takes time for the general congregation to warm up in a Worship service, and starting with thankful, upbeat songs is often the best way to start a service.

People often come to church with their minds on anything but God. A leader's responsibility is to help everyone focus on why they really came to church in the first place. Our main purpose is to meet God. Having a progression in the Worship service can help people set aside other distractions and focus on God.

The term "Praise and Worship" indicates that general trend of transitioning from Praise songs **about** God, to Worship songs that are **to** God, worshipping God directly.

Understand the Importance of Worship in the Bible

The books of Psalms (the largest book in the Bible) is a songbook. There are songs sprinkled throughout the Bible. Some of the greatest men of God were songwriters: Moses, David and Solomon were among the most prolific.

God is looking for people to worship Him.

Jesus said, "But the hour is coming, and is now, when the true worshippers will worship the Father in spirit and truth, for the Father seeks such as those to worship Him. God is spirit, and those who worship Him must worship in spirit and truth."

John 4:23-24

God loves worshippers! King David was called *"a man after God's own heart"* (see 1 Samuel 13:14; also Acts 13:22). He was also one of the chief song-writers of the Bible and a man who loved to worship God.

And David danced before the LORD with all his might, wearing a priestly garment. So David and all the people of Israel brought up the Ark of the LORD with shouts of joy and the blowing of rams' horns.

1 Samuel 6:14-15

In spite of his failures, David's desire was to be close to God, and Worship was one of his best ways to express that. Worship – specifically, musical Worship – is important to God. Never underestimate what God can do through anointed musicians and great songs of Worship.

Learn a Musical Instrument

Most Worship leaders play an instrument. It is not a prerequisite, but it is of great help. The two main instruments for a leader are the guitar and the keyboard. Piano generally takes longer to become proficient, so I suggest people who take up an instrument later in life should take up the guitar. Obviously, the earlier in life we start playing an instrument, the better chance we have at being proficient.

Another great way to learn is just to listen and imitate the Worship songs we want to learn. Take it note by note, chord by chord, and learn to listen to what the keyboard or guitar player is playing.

This is often the most effective way of learning, once we accomplish the basic playing level of an instrument. Copying the players on professional recordings will teach us a better rhythm and help us learn a variety of styles. It will also help develop our ability to play by ear.

Learn to Sing to the Best of Our Ability

Singing is a big part of leading. We do not have to be an awesome singer to lead Worship, but the more acceptable our tone, pitch and vibrato are, the less distracting it is to the congregation. The opposite can also be true: great singers sometimes do not make good Worship leaders. They are often too busy vocalizing to facilitate the average singer in the congregation.

Leaders should generally just sing the melody. The leader's voice is usually highest in the vocal mix, and if we sing harmonies, it could throw off weaker singers in our congregation. It is okay to throw in an *ad lib* occasionally, but do not let it become a distraction. Learning to *ad lib* in the various musical forms is an art; use good taste and discretion, and listen to recordings of ourselves.

Learn a Variety of Different Song Styles

"Variety is the spice of life." A congregation appreciates variety. The tastes of most congregations represent a huge spectrum of music: Pop, Rock, Rhythm and Blues, Country, Folk, Irish, Classical, *Ballade,* Jewish, Gospel, and Alternative among the many styles that can be used in Worship services. Putting the right style with the right song can bring the song to life. Learning new styles, rhythm feels, chord progressions, and vocals are great ways to grow musically. Don't get stuck in a rut.

Music is constantly changing, and we should grow and change with it. God is not limited to "a style." Classical-styled Worship music is not more spiritual than Pop- or Rock-styled Worship music. It's the lyrics and the heart of the musicians that define the spiritual depth of a song.

Learn to Communicate in Front of Your Congregation

Effective communication comes in many forms. The way we speak, act and dress all communicate volumes to our congregations. Learning to speak in public is difficult for many people. Polls indicate that speaking in public is the greatest fear for many people. Worship leaders are not required to speak volumes, but the right words at the right time are very effective.

Worship leaders should always remember that they aren't the preacher. Some of the most effective Worship leaders speak very little.

Learn to overcome such problems as stuttering, or talking to fast. Learn to speak clearly and succinctly. Learn good grammar, and don't get in the habit of using too many clichés. Saying "*Amen*" and "*Hallelujah*" every second word usually shows insecurity on the part of the speaker.

Humility in a Worship leader is of paramount importance. We cannot fake humility, at least not for very long. Our body language will speak volumes to the congregation. If they see a Worship leader and team who are totally yielded to and passionate about God, they will be more open to that leadership.

Leading with a humble spirit **and** authority is an important balance in effective leadership. People can usually detect when we're "just going through the motions" or when we are truly passionate about God – we can inspire and encourage people on, and we can turn people off.

The style of clothing we wear is also relevant to the message we are sending to the congregation. The best questions to ask are: *"What fits best in the situations?"* and *"What will be the least distracting from my main purpose of glorifying God?"* The key is to be relevant to the congregations we are leading. Don't let our clothes be a distraction for our ministry. My general rule-of-thumb is to dress one notch higher than what the general congregation wears to church.

Learn to Work Well With Our Pastors

A church will only rise to the level of its pastor. If our pastors are worshippers, the church will soon follow. Developing a good working relationship and understanding between the pastor and the Worship leader is extremely important. If they do not share the same vision, neither vision will be accomplished; they will always be pulling in different directions.

It is helpful to meet at least once a week with the Pastor, to review the last Sunday's services, and then plan for the next week's and the weeks to come. It is also good to meet occasionally in informal situations (coffee, lunch, sports activities, etc.) to continue to develop a good relationship. The Senior Pastor and the Worship

Leader are usually the most visible in public ministry. If they do not work well together, then the opposite can be true.

There are number of ways a Pastor can facilitate Worship in a church; one is by regularly teaching on Worship. The Bible is full of great passages on Worship. If the Pastor is not comfortable teaching on Worship, there a number of good books on the subject from which to gather resource material.

Another important way for a Pastor to facilitate Worship is to model it. If the Pastor is a wholehearted worshipper, the congregation will take their cues from him. These days, the lead Pastor doesn't generally sit on the platform, but it is still important for him to be a passionate worshipper from wherever he sits in the congregation.

Worship leading is a great privilege and challenge. It is great to be able to point people to God through Worship. Learn to grow in our singing, playing and leading. Learn to hear God's Spirit as we lead. Be passionate in our love-relationships with God, and for the people in our Worship team and congregation.

37: STARTING A YOUTH WORSHIP BAND

Recently I was asked to give advice on how to start a Youth Worship Band. One of the churches I worked at had a small private Christian school, and I was put in charge of working with their school-aged Worship team. I worked with that team for a number of years, and they all became very good. In fact, when I was doing para-church ministry, they were often the group I took as my band. Today, several of them are very good leaders.

Here is what I learned through the process.

Have the Kids Take Private Lessons

Of the core group I inherited, more than half took private lessons. Two brothers had taken private electric guitar lessons; they became quite strong players. The drummer and the piano player also took lessons, and improved immensely over the course of 3 to 4 years. When the leader doesn't have to teach the basics on the instruments, everyone moves along exponentially faster. We only have to teach the music, not the instrument.

I would help the drummer understand the groove I needed. I wrote out and played piano riffs I needed the keys player to learn. I would still help the guitar players understand the lead lines and strumming patterns they needed to play. Since the kids were taking Music lessons, they had some basic skills I could help them build upon.

I also taught an acoustic guitar class. It was great to see kids from that class develop their skills quite quickly, and then join the Worship team. I highly recommend encouraging parents to get private lessons for their kids. At the least, have your older players come in and set up some kind of mentoring system.

Run Separate Rehearsals For Vocals

Most young singers are not that good at picking out harmonies. I would write out vocal parts, and have separate rehearsals with the vocals. My general pattern was to put the song in a good key for the male voice. The top note would be a C# or D, and the guys would sing the melody. I would stack the harmonies (two or three parts) on top of that, with girls on tenor and alto parts.

Then I would give the kids the written music, and teach them the parts by singing through them. After awhile, they became quite good at following along and picking out their parts.

I actually had a large group of students singing in my vocal class. Then I would have auditions for singing on the actual Worship team. My experience is that only about 10% of students are actually musical enough to be on a Worship team.

Rehearse As Much As You Can

Since this group was in a Christian school, I ended up having three separate rehearsals per week with them. First, the one-hour vocals-only rehearsal; second, the one-hour band plus vocals rehearsal; and then a rehearsal just before Chapel, to work on the flow, worship and performance details.

That school team also became the backbone of the Youth Worship Team. That meant they would also rehearse one night per week, then lead for the youth services. This gave them the chance to grow on their own. It also meant they were doing Worship music a minimum of three to four hours per week. As they became older, they also joined my Sunday team, which added more experience and time spent playing, singing and worshipping.

Repeat the Music on a Regular Rotation

I taught two new songs per month, and had a regular rotation for the music. I would teach the new song on week one, repeat it on week two, give it a rest for week three, then bring it back for week four. That helped the Chapel group really learn the songs, and also helped the student body learn to be confident with the Worship songs. We did only three songs per week in Chapel. That gave us time to really work on those three tunes.

Teach the Team About Stage Presence and Worship

I would frequently encourage the kids about getting over their stage-fright. When we are young, it is often a little frightening to be up in front of our peers. We would talk about this, and I would tell stories of my triumphs and failures, so they would understand how common this is for most people.

I explained and modeled how important it is to be an example in Worship. They learned where I wanted them to clap, or raise their hands. They were frequently reminded to smile, and to look at the student body, congregation or audience they were leading in Worship. The singers were also encouraged to memorize the lyrics.

Bring New Leaders Along Slowly

For many years, I would lead most of the Worship times. Then when I was away, I would often schedule one of the kids to lead. When I came back, I would find out what worked and what didn't, and helped them learn from the process.

The goal was for them to always be successful. They were given the tools, rehearsals, music, systems, and experience so that Worship would be a fun experience. They received the support they needed so they could grow in confidence.

Challenge Them to Be Excellent

My toughest teachers were those who helped me grow and learn fastest, so I learned to be a little tough with kids. In rehearsals, I challenged them when they sang flat or missed cues; challenged them to concentrate and to play to the best of their ability. I expected them to be excellent.

It is important to quickly read the characters and personalities of different students. Learn when to be tough and when to be patient. Learn to sense when kids are struggling for personal reasons or are just being lazy. Challenging kids to be their best really is the optimal way to achieve maximum results. Trust me: it works.

38: ACTIONS SPEAK SO LOUDLY

Years ago, I learned the old proverb "*Actions speak louder than words*" was true. If people hear us saying or singing one thing but our actions are speaking another thing, they tend to believe our actions rather than our words.

I am in love with the Creator of the Universe. He has given me a full and abundant life. He has given me health, has forgiven everything I ever did wrong, has answered my prayers for a great wife and family, and has given me an awesome purpose in life. He supplies my daily needs, and is my closest Friend. He gives me wisdom, peace and love on a daily basis. On top of that, I know He is always with me.

When I worship God in a private or public setting, I want my actions to match my words. I want the people whom I lead in Worship to know – beyond a shadow of a doubt – that I love the Lord with all my heart, soul, mind, and strength. I do not want actions for action's sake – I want to do the Worship-actions of the Bible because they reflect the passion of my heart!

I read the Psalms daily. Throughout the Psalms there are action words. Years ago I decided I wanted my life to line up with God's

Word. I did not want to live my life according to how I think it should be lived – I want to follow a higher wisdom than mine. My desire is to live my life and to worship God according to God's patterns and standards.

God created me. God designed me. I have learned that His ways are superior to my ways. When I worship, I try to worship according to the Biblical pattern, not according to my personal taste, preference or traditions.

Here are the actions of Worship that I have discovered in the Bible:

Singing

God loves singing. The prophet Zephaniah says:

God rejoices over you with joyful singing.
Zephaniah 3:17

Singing is mentioned throughout the Bible. The Psalmist said it this way:

I will sing to the LORD as long as I live. I will praise God to my last breath.
Psalm 104:33 and 146:2

Another Psalmist tell us:

Come into His presence with singing!
Psalm 100:2

In the New Testament, Paul tells us:

Sing psalms and hymns and spiritual songs, with thankfulness in your hearts to God.
Ephesians 5:19 and **Colossians 3:16**

Singing is one of the staple actions of Worship.

Playing Instruments

I love to play instruments. I play around 12 different instruments, so I love that the Bible says playing instruments is an action of Worship.

Psalm 150 is the most famous of the Psalms on this subject.

Praise the LORD! Praise God in His sanctuary; praise Him in His mighty Heaven. Praise Him for His mighty works; praise His unequaled greatness. Praise Him with a blast of the ram's horn; praise Him with the lyre and harp. Praise Him with the tambourine and with dancing; praise Him with strings and flutes. Praise Him with the clash of cymbals, praise Him with loud

clanging cymbals.   Let everything that breathes sing praises to the LORD! Praise the LORD!
Psalm 150

Lifting of Hands

I love what the prophet Jeremiah wrote:

Let us lift our hearts and hands to God in Heaven.
Lamentations 3:41

There is something very spiritual and special about lifting our hands in worship to God.

I love it when my grandkids come to me with their hands lifted toward me: they want me to lift them up and give them a hug. I also love it when I am at a great football game and my favorite team scores ... and the whole crowd jumps to its feet, lifting their hands and shouting. Lifting our hands seems to be a very natural human response.

God loves it when we lift our hands to Him. Many great men of the Bible – like David, Solomon, Ezra, Moses, Paul, and Peter – all lifted their hands in worship and adoration to God.

Clapping

Clapping is another natural human response. We clap in approval at a great musical or sporting event. We clap in time with music. I love to clap intricate rhythms to entertain myself. The Psalms puts it succinctly:

Come, everyone, clap your hands!

Psalm 47:1

Shouting

I have found that people naturally shout in sporting events, in fun times, and in other exciting human endeavors. But somehow they don't think we should shout in church. I serve a God Whose majesty and power are unparalleled. He made the sun, moon and stars; He made all the galaxies. He created this wonderful planet which we so enjoy visiting and exploring. He is interested and involved in the details of my life. Jesus said that *"even the hairs on my head are numbered"* (see Matthew 10:30 and Luke 12:7). Let me tell you: God is more than worthy of my shouts of His praise.

Do you know there is shouting in Heaven? It says in Revelation:

*And I saw a strong angel, who **shouted with a loud voice,** "Who is worthy to break the seals on this scroll and open it?" ...*

And they sang a new song with these words: "You are worthy to take the scroll and break its seals and open it. For You were slaughtered, and Your blood has ransomed people for God, from every tribe and language and people and nation." ... And they sang in a mighty chorus: "Worthy is the Lamb Who was slaughtered, to receive power and riches and wisdom and strength and honor and glory and blessing!"

Revelation 5:2, 9, 12; emphasis added

There are certain times when we should get very excited about God, excited about what He has done and is doing, that the only natural human response should be to shout! God doesn't want us to be inhibited when it comes to our praise to Him. Jesus said:

If we don't praise Him, even the rocks and stones will cry out!

Luke 10:40

Dancing

Dancing is another of those human responses that many people aren't comfortable with in church. To tell you the truth: I am a musician with a good sense of rhythm, but I am not a good dancer. Fortunately, God still loves it when I express my joy before Him with my own kind of dancing. (Don't worry about it – we are dancing to celebrate Him, not to impress each other.)

David was uninhibited when it came to expressing his joy in the Lord with dancing. Even when he became king, his joy overflowed into dancing. Women seem to be freer in expressing themselves in dance than men. Frankly, I feel a little awkward when I dance, but as Solomon said,

> *There is a time to weep, and a time to laugh; a time to mourn, and a time to dance.*
> **Ecclesiastes 3:4**

Bowing Down

Bowing down in Worship seems to be more of an accepted Eastern practice than a Western one. Personally, I have only used bowing down just a few times in a corporate Worship setting. In my private worship, I have used it more often.

Sometimes, God makes His presence known in an awesome way, and the only acceptable way to worship Him is to bow down. He is the King of Kings and the Lord of Lords. When we become aware that we are in the presence of the Creator of the Universe, it only seems appropriate to get own on our knees before our Lord and bow before Him.

The Psalmist said it this way:

Come, let us worship and bow down. Let us kneel before the LORD our Maker, for He is our God.

Psalm 95:6

Standing

I love it when congregations stand and worship God. They sing better, are more attentive, and are more involved. It's not that you can't worship God when you are sitting, it's just that people sing, clap, lift their hands, and praise God with more enthusiasm when they stand.

The Apostle John had a glimpse of worship in Heaven:

*After this I saw a vast crowd, too great to count, from every nation and tribe and people and language, **standing** in front of the Throne and before the Lamb. They were clothed in white robes and held palm branches in their hands. And they were **shouting** with a great roar: "Salvation* *comes from our God Who sits on the Throne, and from the Lamb!"*

Revelation 7:9-10; emphasis added

I love that picture! This huge, multi-ethnic crowd is standing and shouting their praise to God in Heaven. How cool is that!

Giving

Years ago I memorized Romans 12. In the first verse, it says:

Dear brothers and sisters, I urge you to give your bodies to God because of all that He has done for you. Let your lives be a living and holy sacrifice – the kind He will find acceptable. This is truly the way to worship Him.

Romans 12:1

I believe that giving our whole lives to God is the most important way to worship Him. God loves it when we trust Him enough to lay down our goals and desires, and offer our lives to Him.

Can we trust God enough to give Him our goals, our finances, our dreams? Can we trust Him enough to die to our own ambitions, and let Him live through us? Can we trust Him to do a better job with our lives than we can? I do.

39: WAYS TO IMPROVE WORSHIP TEAMS

Great teams always start with great leaders. Leadership is crucial. What are we doing as leaders to improve? Here are some areas to look at when we are working on improving our leadership and our teams. Generally speaking, teams never rise above their leader.

Model Worship

If we are passionate and biblical worshippers, it will rub off on our teams.

(a) **How is our passion for God?** God is the Source of all good things. He is the Source of creativity, the Source of wisdom, the Source of joy. How much time are we spending with the Source? How much time are we spending with our Creator?

Are we reading our Bibles daily? Are we encouraging and challenging our teams to read their Bibles daily? There are several daily Bible reading programs available online; I recommend starting with a reading program that will eventually take you through the entire Bible chronologically in a year. An entire team reading the same Bible reading program can be very mutually rewarding and can change lives. It will take only about 15 minutes per day.

Personally, I believe it is good to read one Psalm and one Proverb per day. The Psalms are must-reads for musicians, and the Proverbs teaches us how to deal with people.

Are we praying on a regular basis? No matter how busy Jesus was, He got away from the crowds and spent time with God. We all need time with God! We do not need to do a lot of talking – simply find some quiet place and spend time with Him. Make lists of things we are praying about, and check them off as God answers our prayers.

(b) **How is our understanding of Biblical Worship?** True Worship includes singing, playing an instrument, clapping hands, shouting, bowing. It is passionate and reverent, and often contagious.

(c) **How is our stage presence?** Video ourselves and our teams and play it back together, noting when focus faltered or glitches occurred – and when we connected with the congregation and sensed God's presence strongly. It is always good to work with our teams and remind them to be passionate worshippers. Getting a team to smile is huge! There is great power in smiling. It can change the mood of an entire congregation.

Model Excellence

If we model excellence, it will slowly rub off on our teams.

(a) **Personal practice** – Are we putting in the consistent daily time to be the best singers and players we can be? Are we encouraging our teams to put in regular practice time? Are we and our teams better this year than we were last year ... or have we plateaued?

(b) **Memorization** – Are we taking the time to memorize the music every week? Are we encouraging our teams to memorize their music? Memorization helps to get the songs into our spirits, and it really helps us and our teams communicate with the congregation at a higher level. There's nothing worse than having a leader and team who are just reading music on a Sunday morning.

(c) **Always learning** – Have **we** improved our organizational skills this year? Are we reading and growing? What other skills have we improved on this past year?

(d) **Learning to change and grow** – Music is constantly changing. Musical forms are changing, chord progressions are changing, chord voicings are changing. Rhythms and grooves are changing. Are we listening to the new music and learning to change with it? Are we staying fresh and growing?

(e) **Private lessons** – Have we thought about taking private lessons? Are we challenging our teams to take lessons? What can we do to improve our singing and playing?

(f) **Personal grooming** – Are our personal grooming habits changing with the times? How are our haircuts and hairstyles? Is the style of our clothing relevant to the people to whom we are ministering? I'm not talking about being trendy, just current. Is our look dated? Are we presenting the image to our congregations that helps them engage in Worship?

(g) **Written standards** – Do we have written guidelines for our teams? When we have our expectations written down, it solves a lot of misunderstanding.

Great Songs

Sometimes a team does not do well because the songs are not as strong as they could be. Great songs make leading Worship easy. Compare your list with *CCLI's SongSelect Top 200*. It will help to see if we are on track.

Listening

What we listen to invades our hearts, sometimes without us even realizing it has done so.

(a) **Personal listening** – To what music are we listening? Are we stuck with one group or one church stream? Or do we listen to a good variety of music from different parts of the world? Again, *CCLI's SongSelect Top 200* is a good place to start. Personally, that list helps me know what the main musical flow is across the Body of Christ around the whole world. It is easier than ever to go to *iTunes* and pick the top songs from the new albums that are coming out. We should have a "music listening" budget-item and buy new music all the time.

(b) **Team listening** – Are we encouraging our teams to listen to new music? Are we putting on the current music online for the new songs we are learning? Are we giving our teams links to the *YouTube* recordings and videos of the songs we are using? I put the MP3s online, and also send *YouTube* links to the songs we are using that week.

(c) **Learning to listen** – Are we and our teams really listening to what is happening in the songs? Are we listening to the new rhythm patterns the drums, bass and guitars are doing? Are we really listening to the new sounds the electric guitar and keyboards are using? Are we listening to vocal inflections, harmonies and riffs? Is this careful listening reflected in what our teams are playing and singing?

Great Rehearsals

(a) **On time** – Are we on time? Do we arrive early and have everything ready to go? I expect (and I demand) that my team is on time. This sets the tone for the whole rehearsal: when everyone shows up and is ready to go on time.

(b) **Professional attitude** – I work in both professional and volunteer settings. In professional settings, players and singers are expected to learn the material on their own time. They arrive early, and are set-up and ready to go. They come to the rehearsal with the attitude of doing whatever it takes to please the producer. I expect the same work-ethic and attitude from my volunteers.

Great Charts

One of the keys to improving our Worship bands and our rehearsals is to give our groups great charts. The majority of Worship bands' charts fall into one of two camps:

- most use a lyric sheet with the chords on top;
- personally, I prefer a full Rhythm/SAT vocal chart, with all the written notes, solo cues, repeats, with first and second endings, D.S., and Coda.

If we are doing lyric-chord style charts, it is important to double-check the chords and make certain they are all correct. Chord charts downloaded from the Internet often have mistakes. I would also put in the overall form of the songs (i.e. - Intro, V1, C, V2, C, Bridge, C, C, Ending) and chords for the intro, instrumental sections and ending (outro).

The more information we have on our charts, the less time we have to spend in the rehearsal explaining the music to the band.

I have been a professional chart writer and musical arranger for most of my life, so I am quite fussy about my charts. I normally spend four or six hours on each new SAT/Rhythm chart and make it as perfect as I can. I put in written musical cues for the leader, back-vocals, drums, bass, guitars, and keys. Then after the first rehearsal with that chart, I will go home and revise anything that didn't work in the rehearsal.

It is also important to note that some bands just "play by ear." I grew up in this environment. The lead player usually just plays the song, everyone listens and then picks up the music on their own. I think to be a well-rounded musician, we should be able to do all three: improvise off a chord chart, read written notes, and "play by ear."

Vocals

There are a number of different styles of vocals that are popular. The current trend is to have the main leader (usually a man), with one or two backup vocalists (often women) throwing in some occasional two-part harmony. This style is a little more impromptu, and usually gives the singers lots of room to do what they think sounds best for the song. This also works best when rehearsal time is limited, and when the background singers are good at picking out their own parts.

My favorite style is to put the leader on melody, with his top note around a D, and then stack two other parts above that (TSA). I usually save the harmonies for the chorus and the bridge, if it is appropriate. This style works well with one woman singing tenor and another singing the alto part above. This puts all the singers in their strongest vocal ranges.

Another popular style is to have a large group of vocalists (anywhere from six singers, to a full choir), and to have the traditional soprano on the melody, with two parts below (SAT). We can hear examples of this from the *Brooklyn Tabernacle Choir*, or the Worship Team and choir led by Israel Houghton at *Lakewood Church* in Houston.

Of course, we can add a bass part (SATB), or change the vocals around so the men are singing the melody with the ladies singing parts above (TSA), or sandwich the melody between two harmonies (ATB) where a man sings the melody with an alto part above and a bass or baritone part below the melody. Or, if we don't have any males, we could do three-part females (SAA). Or we could all just sing the melody Sunday School-style!

I won't attempt to give a vocal arranging course at this point, but I will say **the vocals are the most important part of any Worship band.** It has been my observation that many groups do not spend enough time working on their vocals.

When I work with vocal sections, I make sure everyone is singing the proper rhythms for the song, are breathing at the best places, memorizes the music, learns to enunciate properly, knows what are the harmonies for the different sections of the song, and learns to blend properly.

Other considerations are mic technique, great stage presence, and worship. I never want the singers – or any of the band, for that matter – to be just singing songs. They must get past the music to singing to the Creator. They must be worshippers and Worship leaders, not just singers.

I also look for singers who worship God whether they are on the stage or off the stage. If people only "worship" on the stage, then something is not quite right. That usually indicates they are performing more than they are worshipping.

The Worship Band Rhythm Section

(1) **The Band** – A Worship band can come in many different shapes and sizes. Most contemporary church Worship bands have a drummer, a bass player, a keyboard player, an acoustic guitar player, and a lead guitar player (a five-piece rhythm section). We can also effectively operate with just three players (bass, drums, and either keys or guitar). To expand to a 7- or 8-piece band, we can add a second keyboard player (synthesizer, B-3 organ, laptop with effects or background track), rhythm electric guitar, and percussion. An even larger band can include a horns section, or a strings section. The general rule is the more players we have, the less busily everyone plays.

I prefer the 7- or 8-piece band because it gives the greatest possible variety. But it also needs more musical direction to make sure everyone is not playing too much. It also depends on the musical forces available in our church settings. For a long time, many churches operated with just a piano player or organist; now, most churches have rhythm sections of various sizes.

(2) **Tempo** – Some of the newer changes to the Worship band setting are the use of in-ear monitors and a click track. This works best with personal monitor mixers (often *Aviom* or *Roland*) for the whole band. The drummer will program different tempos of the Worship set into an advanced metronome, or an App from an *iPad, iPod* or *iPhone,* and feed the click through a channel to the rest of the band. Some bands also use backing tracks with click tracks that fill in extra orchestrations such as strings sections, brass sections, special effects, or other synth sounds.

Click tracks have been a staple of recording studios forever. They are great for helping the band play rhythmically tighter. The challenge is to get the band so used to the "click" that they feel comfortable playing with it, and are also worshipping at the same time. Frankly, I never want to substitute musical perfection for true heart-felt worship. I believe we can have both, but we have to work at it.

Another simple solution for tempo is to have small flashing metronomes on stage for the players (usually the drummer, piano or acoustic guitar) who are starting a particular piece. This gets the music started at the right tempo, then the drummer, band and singers just need to maintain that tempo.

(3) **Musical Feel** – Nothing changes the musical feel or groove of a song like the "kick-and-snare" of the drums (i.e. - bass drum and snare drum). We don't have to *be* drummers to lead the band, but we should know the basic "kick-and-snare" grooves. We should make notes of what beats the bass drum is on. Normally the kick is on some variation of "one and three"... sometimes it is on every beat ... sometimes it is "one-and two-and" ... and occasionally there is no kick at all for certain sections of a song.

The same applies to the snare. Sometimes it is on "two and four" ... or a "half-time feel on three" ... or the snare is every beat. And sometimes there is no snare at all for certain sections of the music.

Often a musical groove will change from the verse to the chorus, to the bridge. It is usually very boring to have the same groove throughout a whole song. The leader and band should know when the groove changes.

We should grow familiar with terms like "four on the floor" (kick every beat, with snare on "two and four") ... "shuffle" (triplet eighth feel)

... "sixteenth feel" ... "half-time feel" ... "double-time Country" ... and "Rock." There are a myriad of types of musical feels in general, but most contemporary Christian music uses more Rock, Pop, Country, and Gospel feels.

There are new terms being invented all the time as music grows and changes. If we don't a term, ask our drummers or other experienced players. Also, sometimes bands and players have different names for the same groove.

(4) **Musical layering and dynamics** – Another important area leaders should note is where the different instruments and vocals come in and out. A general rule is that we want the song to build. Having all instruments play all the time gets musically boring.

We want to build musical variety and dynamics into a song by changing up the vocals and band instrumentation. Sometimes it will be acoustic guitar or piano only, sometimes it will be bass and drums only. Often the electric guitar will lay out a softer verse, then come in with more power to the chorus. Normally the whole band is in by the first or second chorus. Sometimes there is an *a cappella* section (vocals only) with drums.

Noting all those details from the original recording or adding your own musical ideas will help bring variety into the arrangement.

(5) **Stage layout** – I was on the road for years playing in different auditoriums, churches and stages every night. It was amazing how creative we had to get with the band set-up every evening! Here are some general "rules."

If possible, put the drums toward the back of the stage in the center. They are the heartbeat of the band, and the nearer the band is to the drummer, the easier it is to play as one unit. Having said that, I have put drummers in baptismal tanks, in sound cages, at stage right, at stage left, and on the floor in front of the singers. With different stage set-ups, set decor, large video screens, and choir lofts, we sometimes need to get very creative.

Another rule is to have good sight-lines between the leader and drummer. If the drummer can't clearly see the leader, there will usually be musical problems. It is also important to put the bass player next to the drummer. They need to communicate and provide the musical feel for the band. The closer they are together, the better their communication.

The most important visual feature is the Worship leader and singers. Of course, they should be well-lit, and at the front and center of the stage.

(6) **Stage presence** – It is important for the band to have great stage presence. Ideally, they should memorize their music, and sing and worship during the set. For the music and Worship to be all it should be, musicians who are also worshippers is huge. If the band is totally into the music and also worshipping God, it really creates a great setting to lead the congregation in Worship.

A few players will naturally have good stage presence but, frankly, most musicians can be shy on stage. As leaders, we must continually encourage our whole bands to worship onstage. Seeing the whole band worshipping is important to the overall Worship experience. Genuine and heart-felt Worship is powerful.

The last installment to improving our Worship teams is about that important techie who helps us sound good.

Sound

This is the person who can make or break us. Excellent church sound people are worth their weight in gold! I have worked with a whole range of sound men. (In the following – as with all these discussions of bands and singers – I am choosing here to write about a male, but sound people may also be female.)

(1) Here are the qualities of the top sound men which I appreciate the most.

(a) **He is a nice person.** He shows up on time, he has a servant's heart, he smiles, he encourages, he is patient, and he doesn't get uptight.

(b) **He understands technical stuff.** When something goes wrong, he becomes a detective and works through the problems until he finds a solution. He keeps up with the changing technology, and he is constantly figuring out how to do the techie stuff better.

(c) **He has good ears.** He hears when something is not right. He understands musical balance and mixing. He understands how to get a comfortable mix for the congregation.

(d) **He has thick skin.** A church sound person will always be criticized. There are such a huge range of personal preferences in the congregation that it is impossible to please everyone.

(2) Ways to help our sound men:

(a) During rehearsals, ask our bands to direct all their sound requests through one person. In my case, that is always me, the leader.

(b) Decide on a decibel level that works best for our congregations, auditorium and staff. Get our lead Pastors and staff to agree on a level, and then get back to and support the sound man when he gets complaints (which he always will). My preference is to run it a strong level so the congregation is comfortable with singing loudly. Our main goal is to always get maximum participation from the congregation. Whatever level helps get that result is – in my opinion – the best level to run for my congregation.

(c) During rehearsals, ask the sound man if there is anything the band can do to make the mix better.

(d) Teach the singers how to use the microphones properly. Teach them to sing at a consistent level, and how to back off the mic if they suddenly increase their volume.

(e) Have the band and singers practice at the same volume and intensity during rehearsals as the service.

(f) Get to know him as a person, not just as sound men. Express gratitude to him on a regular basis. Find ways to reward him for all his hard work.

(g) Pay for any training or seminars that will help him grow.

(3) **Room Acoustics** – This is a huge subject, but I will address just a few areas.

(a) **The drums** – There are basically two ways to control the volume of drums. First, leave it to the drummers to play at the perfect volume; second, put them in a sound-proof drum cage – either expensive, medium or homemade – and mic them up. Personally, I prefer the second scenario, which gives complete control to the sound man. The drummer can play at the level they prefer, and the sound man can run their level best for the room. Win-win! [For more, check out Carl Albrecht's advice: http://carlalbrecht.com/2011/12/the-dreaded-drum-booth/]

(b) **The bass** – Bass waves are long sound waves. If the bass player's amplifier is too close, he often can't hear his volume properly. The best way to control the volume is either to put baffles around the amp and point the amp at the bass player. Or have the player wear in-ear monitors or headsets.

(c) **Natural room acoustics** – My advice is to hire professionals and do whatever it takes to make the room work. It will often be a trial-and-error process. It is usually an art rather than a science to get a room to work acoustically.

(4) **Media Person:** I love a media person who knows the songs backwards and forwards, and worships while she is operating the media. The media person needs to rehearse as much as the band. They are an integral part of the overall Worship experience.

I usually run two different media set-ups: one for the congregation; and another rear-mounted set-up for the vocalists. The vocalists don't need all the fancy graphics – they just need clear black-on-white lyrics that are delivered just before they need them. Many of the new media programs are designed to deliver that duel design.

I love the ability to run triple-wide graphics and multiple screens. People are accustomed to big screens in their homes and at the theater. It is great to have strong graphics and professional media set-ups.

(5) **Ways to help our media persons:**

(i) Buy a great computer with lots of RAM. Nothing is worse than a slow computer. My favorite is a top-of-the-line *Mac* that has lots of memory and RAM.

(ii) Have all the media set up midweek so she only has to come in and run it Sunday morning.

(iii) Put the lyrics slides in the order we will sing them. We want to make the set-up foolproof.

(iv) Practice the songs, including any reprises, at the rehearsal the same way we will do them in the services. The less we surprise the media person, the better chance she has of doing a great job!

(v) Love the media person, encourage her, challenge her, and give her all the tools and training she needs to do a great job.

(6) **Lighting** – Good lighting and lighting boards cost money. I believe every church should invest in these basics. There should be enough lighting so we can see the faces of the Worship team and the speaker.

Beyond that, the sky is the limit. It's always a matter of where is the best place to spend available finances. Personally, I want to make sure the stage and lighting are the best our church can afford. It's all about creating a great first impression.

On the other side of the issue, lighting does not bring the Presence of God. It just makes the whole place look better when God shows up.

Teach on Worship

One way we disciple our Worship teams is to teach them about Worship. *"What does the Bible say? How are we to worship? What is Biblical worship?"*

(1) **Bible reading and prayer** – Encourage everyone in our teams to read our Bibles regularly. It's a good thing to read together a daily Bible plan. Also read one Psalm and one Proverbs per day. It's a great way to round out our daily Bible reading.

It is also important for our teams to pray together regularly. My practice has been to pray at the end of the rehearsal and also together on Sunday mornings.

40: FINALE – THE MOST IMPORTANT FACTS ABOUT WORSHIP

Years ago, I realized I often had only one shot at communicating with an audience in some of the countries I visited. So I asked myself, *"If I can only speak once to an audience, what are the most important things on Worship I can share?"* Here are my top five most important facts about Worship:

1. **God wants us to worship Him** – Jesus said so:

> *"The hour is coming and is already here when the true worshippers will worship the Father in spirit and truth; for the Father is looking for those who will worship Him that way."*
> **John 4:23-25**

God wants us to worship Him. **He wants you to worship Him.** God is happy when we live good lives but He wants more than that: He is looking for worshippers. He is looking for people who are in love with Him. In fact, they are so in love with Him that they long to be in His presence and worship Him.

2. **Worship is one of the most important ways of loving God** – The greatest commandment is to

love the Lord with all we have. Again quoting Jesus, He said:

> "*Love the Lord your God with all your heart and with all your soul and with all your mind and with all your strength.*"

Mark 12:30

Worship is a natural outflow of our love for God. Let me give you an example from my marriage. I love my wife, so I try to do things that she likes:

- Once a week, I take Anna out for breakfast or dinner because she loves to go out – *even though I prefer her cooking at home.*
- I buy Anna flowers because she loves them – *even though they can be expensive and last only 3 to 5 days.*
- I buy Anna perfume – *okay, this is a win-win because I love it when she smells great!.*
- I try to help Anna around the house without being asked – *I am not always successful at this.*
- I tell Anna daily that I love her – *I am successful at this, although she sometimes forgets that I do it.*

When we love someone, we try to do the things that please them. It is a natural outflow of my love for my wife Anna. I try to do those things with my whole heart. If I grumble and complain when I do them, then they really don't count ... at least, not in my wife's books!

The same principle applies to our worship and love for God: God is looking for worshippers who are willingly worshipping Him with our whole hearts. He is looking for people who are passionate in our love for Him. God is not at all interested in lukewarm love. He does not want 50% or 75% – God wants us to love Him with our whole hearts, souls, minds, and strength.

3. **God wants us to worship Him according to His Word** – To stay with the marriage analogy, if I did things totally my own way, our lives would look quite different.

- For fun, we would go bike riding and play tennis – *but my wife does not like bike riding or tennis.*
- We would eat at home 99% of the time (she is a great gourmet cook) – *but my wife likes to go out once or twice a week.*
- I would pass on helping around the house – *I'm a man ... what can I say?!?*

When we get to know God and His Word, we discover that He likes things done His way. And frankly, His way is always the best way! Jesus said:

"God is Spirit, and those who worship Him must worship in spirit and truth."

John 4:24

(a) **What does it mean to worship God "*in spirit*"?**

God made us with three separate parts to our beings: body, soul and spirit. We can best communicate with God on a spirit-level since *"God is Spirit"* (see John 4:24a). When our spirits connect with God's spirit, that's Worship.

Let me explain how it works for me. When I am leading Worship or I am participating in a Worship service, I can either just sing through the songs or go through the motions **OR** I can really focus my heart on God! When I sing the words and truly mean them from the depths of my being, **that** is when true Worship begins. My spirit begins to connect with God's Spirit.

(b) **What does it mean to worship God "*in truth*"?**

In John 17:17, Jesus said: "*God's Word is truth.*" To worship God according to "truth" is to worship Him according to the patterns in His Word. "What patterns?" The Bible talks about worshipping God by singing ... playing instruments ... lifting hands ... clapping ... shouting ... dancing ... bowing down ... standing ... and giving.

The Bible also talks about our attitudes we should have when we come to Worship. It talks about being thankful ... honest ... reverent ... with faith ... humble ... with joy ... and with our whole hearts.

4. **Singing and worshipping God on Sunday morning is just one facet of Worship** – God wants our love for Him to include more than just Sunday mornings. He wants us to live out our love for Him **on a daily basis.**

God wants us to live daily with thankful hearts:

*Be thankful **in all circumstances**, for this is God's will for you who belong to Christ Jesus.*
1 Thessalonians 5:18; emphasis added

God wants us to do good works and share with the people He brings into our lives:

And don't forget to do good and to share with those in need. These are the sacrifices that please God.

Hebrews 13:16

God wants us to pray regularly:

Pray in the Spirit at all times and on every occasion. Stay alert and be persistent in your prayers for all believers everywhere.

Ephesians 6:18

God wants us to give a portion of our finances regularly:

"Bring all the tithes into the storehouse so there will be enough food in my Temple. If you do," says the LORD of Heaven's Armies, "I will open the windows of Heaven for you. I will pour out a blessing so great you won't have enough room to take it in! Try it! Put Me to the Test!"

Malachi 3:10

God wants us to love our neighbors as ourselves:

"And you must love the Lord your God with all your heart, all your soul, all your mind, and all your strength." The second is equally important: "Love your neighbor as yourself." No other commandment is greater these these.

Mark 12:30-31

Worshipping God should be a daily part of our lives. One way we worship Him is to love those people He has sent into our lives. As we pray for them, help them and share our lives with them, we are pleasing God. When we live a life that is pleasing to Him, He sees it as Worship.

5. **The heart of worship is surrendering your life to God** – The Apostle Paul said:

Give yourselves to God ... surrender your whole being to Him to be used for righteous purposes.

Romans 6:13

So then, my friends, in view of God's great mercy to us, offer yourselves as a living sacrifice to God, dedicated to His service and pleasing Him. This is the true worship that you should offer.

Romans 12:1

True Worship comes from a surrendered life. There have been many times when God has asked me to totally surrender my life to Him.

A number of years back, I was at a major crossroads in my life. I had just left church ministry and started to write music full-time for *PraiseCharts.com*. But I was feeling uneasy and unsatisfied. God was working in my heart. He was asking me if I was willing to go wherever He wanted to send me. He was asking me if I was willing to do whatever He asked of me.

I have learned that **when God starts asking those questions, something unusual is about to happen.** I have also learned that God can do a better job with my life than I can. So once again, I surrendered my whole life to Him. A life without reservations, no holds barred, to follow wherever He wanted me to go and to do whatever He wanted me to do.

Within weeks I was leading Worship in Copenhagen, and experiencing the greatest week of ministry of my life! This led to almost seven years of traveling around the world, seeing thousands of people healed and coming to know Jesus. I have learned that totally surrendering to God is the most powerful way to live my life.

One of the great Christian leaders of the 20th century was **Bill Bright,** the founder of *Campus Crusade for Christ.* Through his staff all around the world, the "*Four Spiritual Laws*" tract and the "*Jesus*" film (seen by over four-billion people), more than 150-million people have come to Christ and will spend Eternity in Heaven because of Bill's ministry.

Bill once was asked, "Why did God use and bless your life so much?"

He responded, "When I was a young man, I made a contract with God. I literally wrote it out and signed my name at the bottom. It said: '*From this day forward, I am a slave of Jesus Christ.*' That's why."

Have you ever made a contract like that with God? Or are you still arguing and struggling with God – making excuses or trying to avoid Him by asking endless questions – over His right to do with your life as He pleases? If God is speaking to you, I urge you to surrender to Him. Trust me: it is the best decision you will ever make!

ADDENDUM

Here is a sample form we have required all potential Worship team members submit before auditioning and being accepted to join the Worship team. You are welcome to adapt this to your own application.

EASTSIDE CITY CHURCH WORSHIP MINISTRIES

Personal Profile

Qualifications

- FAITH, FAMILY and FINANCES all strong and in order
- Committed, faithful member of *Eastside City Church*
- Committed to faithfully attend *Eastside Worship* rehearsals
- Excels in musical proficiency

Expectations

- **Excellence**

  - Commitment to giving your best in whatever you do
  - Open to constructive criticism, lessons and improvement

- **Commitment**

  - Submission to the Lord's timing and the leadership's time-frame for your ministry here at *Eastside City Church*
  - Faithfully attend Worship rehearsals
  - Faithful attendance and punctuality to rehearsals, sound checks, events, and private practice time

- **Respect**

  - Pray for our leadership, both at *Eastside* and the Church as a whole
  - Respect and honor the leadership, and submit to the guidelines they have established

- **Growth**

  - Spiritual, relational, skill
  - Pledge to be spiritually prepared to minister (this includes having personal prayer and worship time, while seeking the heart of God)

- **Team Attitude**

  - Be a team player!
  - Grow and flow together with a cooperative attitude

- **Communication**

  - Honorable communication between yourself, leadership and fellow team members
  - Develop healthy relational team dynamics through encouragement and positive exhortation.

By completing this Personal Profile, you are in agreement with the above statements and views.

Signature: _____

* * *

I. *General Information*

Name: _____ **Date:** _____
Address: _____
Home Phone: _____ **Cell Phone:** _____
eMail Address *very important*: _____
Birthday: _____ **Occupation:** _____

II. *Ministry Information*

How long have you been attending *Eastside*? _____

Are you a member of _Eastside_ (have you taken membership class)?

     ❑ **Yes** _If yes, when?_ _____

     ❑ **No**

Previous church home: _____

Reason for leaving last church home? _____

_____

Reference from former pastor: _____

_____

Are you a member of a Small Group?

     ❑ **Yes** _If yes, how long?_ _____

     Who is your Small Group leader? _____

     ❑ **No**

Are you currently serving in any other area to _Eastside Church?_ Please specify: _____

_____

Please select below the area(s) in the Worship ministry in which you are interested in being involved. Check all that apply.

     ❑   **Volunteer Team**

     ❑   **Choir**

     ❑   **Music Production**

     ❑   **Internship**

     ❑   **Platform ministry** (Wednesday/Sunday/Thursday teams)

     ❑   **Other:** _____

In which ministries do you have interest? Check all that apply.

Generational

- ❏ **Nursery**
- ❏ **Children**
- ❏ **Youth**
- ❏ **Young Adults**

Adult Ministries

- ❏ *Eastside* **Small Groups Ministry**
- ❏ **Singles Ministry**
- ❏ **55+ Ministry**
- ❏ **Men's/Women's Ministry**

Other

- ❏ **Sunday Services**
- ❏ **Special Events**
- ❏ **Where needed**

III. *Musical History*

Select below the part/instrument in which you would be participating in an evaluation. *Check only those areas for which you plan to audition.*

- ❏ **Soprano** ❏ **Alto** ❏ **Tenor** ❏ **Lead**
- ❏ **Piano** ❏ **Keyboard** ❏ **Drums**
- ❏ **Percussion**
- ❏ **Bass Guitar** ❏ **Acoustic Guitar** ❏ **Rhythm Electric Guitar** ❏ **Lead Electric Guitar**
- ❏ **Other** *please list all* _____

Please list all musical training and experience. *You may use the back.*

IV. *Personal Ministry Objectives and Experience*

Briefly share your personal testimony. *You may use the back.*

What is your view of Worship? _____
_____
_____

Why do you want to be involved in *Eastside Worship* **platform ministry?** _____
_____

What are your ministry goals? _____
_____

What are your strengths? What are your weaknesses?

  Strengths: _____
  Weaknesses: _____

What are you expecting to receive from *Eastside Worship* **or what kind of experience are you expecting?**
_____
_____

Is there anything in your life that could hinder you from ministering to God or the people at *Eastside City Church?* _____
_____
_____

Do you have any family and/or work conflicts that could keep you from dedicating up to 6 hours per week, if you are scheduled on a platform team? _____
_____

Please list all other ministry experience. *You may use the back.*

ACKNOWLEDGEMENTS

I am a bit overwhelmed when I think of all the people who have helped me on this journey:

I must start with my birth father, **Gordon David "Bud" Cole,** who was an avid amateur musician. Our house was always filled with music and with musical instruments. I recall Dad taking me to an *All-Night Gospel Sing.* He just loved music! He passed away when I was 12, but I know he would have been proud to have a son who spent his life pursuing God and Music.

My mother **Margaret Preston** would be the next person I thank. Mom is also musical; she sang alto in the choir and played the saxophone. She ensured my siblings and I went to our music lessons, and gave us the support and musical instruments we needed to have fun with Music. Mom also made sure we went to church. I remember skipping out of church once to date a girl; Mom was not impressed! Church was important to her; to her credit, all six of we kids love the Lord and are attending church to this day.

Mom married again, to a great man, **Ron Preston.** Dad Preston wasn't musical, but he sure was a great support to Mom and all of the kids.

My siblings **Cheryl Pickens, Lorna Webb, Les Cole, Kevin Preston,** and **Shawn Cole** are a musical bunch. They all play instruments and sing to some degree. I had the joy of leading Worship with two of my brothers this last New Year's Eve, at a large church in the Vancouver area. It was great to sing together as we grew up; we would often pick out harmonies as I drove everyone to church and to kids' clubs, in the family *Volkswagen Beetle*. I am proud of each of them in their own way.

There are many musical mentors and teachers to thank. I started piano lessons when I was a young boy, with **Doug Moody.** He was my Music Pastor at church, and a huge musical influence in my life. I learned so much from him.

Thanks goes to the Christian Band *Living Sound.* I served under three *Living Sound* Music Directors: **James "Jim" Gilbert** (who wrote "*I Love You With the Love of the Lord*"), **Larry Dalton** (Music Director for *Oral Roberts TV*), and **Don Moen** ("*God Will Make a Way,*" *Integrity Music*). Don also taught me to play harmonica and some of my favorite piano licks. These great musicians – Jim, Larry and Don – were all strong influences in my musical journey.

There have been great pastors, evangelists and partners from my journey: **Pastor Reg Layzell** ... **Maureen Gaglardi** ... **Terry Law** ... **Bill Phares** ... **Kirk Duncan** ... **Billy Graham** ... **Alvan Lewis** ... **Don Cantelon** and **Brent Cantelon** ... **Ernie Culley** ... **Ryan Dahl** ... **Charles Ndifon** ... and **Ron Leech.** I always learned a little from every Godly person I worked with on my journey.

Recently, **Jeanne Halsey** surprised me by offering to help write this book. The idea came out of nowhere; I had no idea she was even reading my blog. We had met long ago through her brother **Michael Gossett** (who was on that first *Living Sound* tour), who was gracious to write an endorsement for this book. Jeanne's offer of support was really what solidified my vague notion that there **was** a book in my blog – *"Thank you, Jeanne!"*

Finally, I want to thank **God.** He has always been with me. I met Him personally at age 7, when I accepted the forgiveness that came through His Son Jesus. He has never left me; He has never failed me. His love, forgiveness and faithfulness have been amazing. *"Thank You, God! Your love is overwhelming. You are the reason I live."*

RECOMMENDATIONS

"The God of Miracles: A Danish Journalist Examines Healings in the Ministry of Charles Ndifon" by **Henri Nissen**. Published by *Scandinavia Publishing House,* Copenhagen, Denmark; 2003.

"God Songs," by **Paul Baloche** and **Jimmy & Carol Owens** – Paul Baloche and Jimmy and Carol Owens are experienced and wise songwriters and leaders. I love to learn from people who have been successful over a long period of time. I have also worked with Paul several times; he is the real deal. Together, Paul and the Owenses will give you a solid advice on writing and choosing songs for Worship, and even give you a good music theory lesson.

"Extravagant Worship," by **Darlene Zschech**. Darlene Zschech is another of those very successful and experienced Worship leaders. I was blessed to play with her once, and I've sat in her teaching classes and Worship sets. There is a lot to be learned from this Godly woman.

"Exploring Worship," by **Bob Sorge**. I've worked with Bob Sorge a number of times. This book is a classic on Worship; I highly recommend it.

ABOUT THE AUTHOR

Mark Cole is a Jesus follower, a husband, a father, a grandfather, a Worship Leader, a Pastor, the founding arranger for *PraiseCharts.com*, a squash and tennis player, a blogger, and an outdoor enthusiast. He has spent more than 25 years as a Worship Pastor in several of the largest churches in Canada, and has arranged Worship music for thousands of churches worldwide through the website *PraiseCharts.com*.

Mark has led Worship, taught seminars and directed bands in over 55 countries, working with many different ministries. He has also produced 16 recording projects, has published over 80 songs, plays 12 instruments, and holds a Bachelor of Music degree.

Mark has worked and played with many well-known Worship leaders – including **Paul Baloche ... Don Moen ... Darlene Zschech ... Ron Kenoly ... Alvin Slaughter ... Lamar Boschman ... Bob Fitts ... Brian Doerksen ... Darrell Evans** – and pastors and evangelists – including **Billy Graham ... Kenneth Copeland ... Robert Schuller ... Kathryn Kuhlman ... Terry Law ... Charles Ndifon ... Nicky Cruz ... Dr. Paul Yonggi Cho, Sr.** – and Christian organizations – *PromiseKeepers, Integrity Music, CCLI, Word Music.*

Mark also served as the Music Director, Worship Leader and clinician for the *International Worship Institute* in Dallas, Texas; with *Canada Arise* in Vancouver, Canada; and has led music seminars and consulted for churches around the world. He has recorded four live Worship albums of his own material: *"To You, Lord"* ... *"God Is My Rock"* ... *"Move In This City"* ... and *"Healing In His Hands (Live From Copenhagen)."* He has written more than 70 praise band arrangements of his own songs.

Mark and his wife Anna live in Calgary, Alberta, Canada. Their family is: son **Josh Cole** and daughter-in-law **Sonia Cole**, who live in Toronto, Ontario; and daughter **Stephanie Iverson** and son-in-law **Ryan Iverson**, and grandchildren **Berea** and **Ezra**, who live in Calgary. Mark loves hanging out with his family, leading Worship, playing tennis and squash, riding his mountain and road bicycles, writing music, and working on his blog, *"Following God: Notes ♫ From a Grand Adventure."* Mark is also currently writing another book on stories from his life in music.

ABOUT THE EDITOR

Jeanne Halsey is a lifetime writer. Daughter of renowned missionary-evangelist **Dr. Don Gossett,** Jeanne's writing career has flourished with her specific "gift of ghostwriting," which has benefitted many notable people: **Reinhard Bonnke** ... **Sarah Bowling** ... **U. Gary Charlwood** ... **Frank Colacurcio** ... **Marilyn Hickey** ... **Kurt Langstraat** ... **Danny Ost** ... **Paul Overstreet** ... **Dr. Kim O. Ryan** ... **Cliff Self** ... **Robert Tilton** ... **Steve Watt** ... and many others. She frequently teaches *The School of Creative Christian Writing,* and has published a couple dozen books under her own byline.

"My first knowledge of Mark Cole came in 1973, when he joined the musical missionary team Living Sound, *along with my brothers Michael and Donnie Gossett. Over the years Mark has been a great family friend, and I've respected him for his successful musical career (something very difficult to achieve!). More recently as his* Facebook *friend, I've noticed his posts were inevitably drifting towards a book about leading Worship. It has been my pleasure to come alongside him, to edit and help produce this book."*

Jeanne and her husband Kenneth are active members of *North County Christ the King Community Church* in Lynden, Washington; Kenneth is a regular on the church Worship teams (playing keyboards, trumpet and singing); and Jeanne works with the Audio and Visual teams (running cameras, video directing, managing *ProPresenter*). *"So many things Mark said about team-work when working with Worship Teams is so familiar and true!"*

You can contact Jeanne via e-mail by writing to halseywrite@comcast.net, and catch more of her work at www.halseywrite.com, or at www.lulu.com or www.Amazon.com.

Made in the USA
Middletown, DE
04 June 2018